CONTAGIOUS REPRESENTATION

Contagious Representation

Women's Political Representation in
Democracies around the World

Frank C. Thames and Margaret S. Williams

NEW YORK UNIVERSITY PRESS
New York and London

NEW YORK UNIVERSITY PRESS
New York and London
www.nyupress.org

References to Internet websites (URLs) were accurate at the time of writing.
Neither the author nor New York University Press is responsible for URLs
that may have expired or changed since the manuscript was prepared.

LIBRARY OF CONGRESS CATALOGING-IN-PUBLICATION DATA

Thames, Frank.
Contagious representation : women's political representation in democracies around the
world / Frank C. Thames, Margaret S. Williams.
p. cm.
Includes bibliographical references and index.
ISBN 978-0-8147-8417-4 (hardback)
ISBN 978-0-8147-8419-8 (ebook)
ISBN 978-0-8147-8418-1 (ebook)
1. Women—Political activity. 2. Women in public life. 3. Representative government and
representation. 4. Democratization. I. Williams, Margaret S., Ph.D. II. Title.
HQ1236.T43 2013
305.4—dc23   2012028507

New York University Press books are printed on acid-free paper,
and their binding materials are chosen for strength and durability.
We strive to use environmentally responsible suppliers and materials
to the greatest extent possible in publishing our books.

Manufactured in the United States of America

10 9 8 7 6 5 4 3 2 1

For Kim, Kevin, and Jack

CONTENTS

ACKNOWLEDGMENTS

The authors owe a debt of gratitude to the many individuals who made this project possible. Jan Box-Steffensmeier kindly answered many methods questions. Laron Williams gave us critical advice on several of our statistical models. Melinda Adams gave us excellent feedback on earlier versions of our study. Both Lauren Bell and David Williams provided feedback on the initial proposal. Dennis Patterson and the Department of Political Science at Texas Tech University kindly provided us with the resources to make this book possible. Justin Carter compiled the index and ably proofread the final manuscript. Portions of this project were presented at several conferences over the years, and we benefited enormously from the questions and critiques of the discussants, panel participants, and audience members at those conferences. A special thank-you should be given to our editor, Ilene Kalish, and to her assistant, Aiden Amos, for their belief in and assistance with this work.

Frank would like to think his wife, Kim, who patiently put up with the peaks and valleys of the writing process. He would also like to thank Robert Moser, who several years ago suggested exploring gender research. Frank thanks Margie not only for suggesting the idea that led to this book but for putting up with his wild musings and typos. Frank also would like to thank many colleagues in the Department of Political Science at Texas Tech University who provided help and assistance during the writing of the book and who created a helpful, scholarly atmosphere that made writing this book much easier.

Margie would like to thank her husband, Kevin Scott, for providing countless hours of support while this project was under way. She would also like to thank her son, Jack, for waiting until the manuscript was drafted to arrive. Margie would like to thank Lauren Bowen for getting her interested in gender politics. Larry Baum and Kira Sanbonmatsu provided incredibly helpful advice about the book-writing process. The Federal Judicial Center has been very supportive of her research efforts both within and outside the Center. Finally, Margie would like to thank Frank for not laughing at her when she approached him with the idea of studying the influence of contagion on representation or for when she suggested they turn their study into a book.

The authors received enormous support and help from numerous friends and colleagues during this process. Of course, any errors and omissions are the fault of the authors themselves.

CONTAGIOUS REPRESENTATION

1

Women's Political Participation and the Influence of Contagion

We are currently experiencing the greatest level of women's political representation the world has ever seen. Women constituted 18 percent of members of parliaments in 2009 (Inter-Parliamentary Union 2009). Since 2000, twenty-seven women have achieved executive office worldwide (see Jalalzai 2008). Twenty-three percent of the seats on national high courts are now held by women (Williams and Thames 2008). In addition, political parties, mostly due to quota laws, are seeing greater participation by women than at any time in the past (Caul 1999, 2001; Thames and Williams 2010).

The global increase in women's representation in multiple areas is readily apparent in Figure 1.1, which plots the average of women's representation in legislatures, the number of national quotas, the number of female chief executives, and the number of voluntary party quotas in our sample of 159 democracies from 1945 through 2006. In all cases, we can clearly see a general increase in the number of female legislators and executives, as well as in the use of gender quotas at both the national and the party levels.

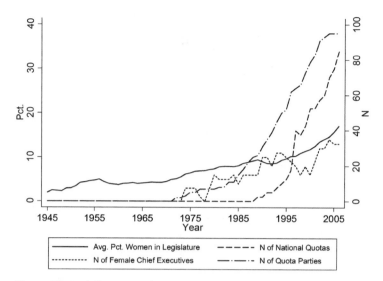

Fig. 1.1. Women's Representation, 1945–2006

This global increase in women's representation is encouraging; however, it is problematic for at least two reasons. First, while we have seen an increasing level of women's representation, we can by no means conclude that we have reached gender parity in the world's democratic institutions. The fact that, in 2009, the average level of women's representation in legislatures was 18 percent is laudable only given the historic underrepresentation of women in such bodies. Second, this global increase in women's representation masks the significant variation among different democratic political systems. In December 2009, women made up 56.3 percent of the members of Rwanda's legislature, while for the U.S. Congress the figure was only 16.8 percent (Inter-Parliamentary Union 2009). Other consolidated democracies maintained similarly weak levels of women's representation (Japan's Diet, for example, is 11.3 percent female), whereas some new democracies feature significantly higher levels of female membership (South Africa's African National Congress is 44.5 percent female, and Mexico's Congress is 28.2 percent female). Related differences in the level of women's representation among executives, judges, and members of political parties are apparent.

Explanations for this variation among countries, in particular in the area of women's legislative representation, have focused on several key factors. For some researchers, differences in political culture are the reason (e.g., Inglehart and Norris 2003). Put simply, the cultures of some countries place a higher value on gender equality, which translates into greater women's representation. Other observers highlight the role of economic factors, in particular women's labor force participation (e.g., Norris 1985; Rule 1987). The presence of more women in the workforce translates into greater women's mobilization, creating a more positive atmosphere for increasing women's representation. In addition, many scholars focus on the effects of political institutions, in particular electoral systems and gender quotas (e.g., Kittilson 2006; Matland 1993; Salmond 2006).

While the existing work forms a solid foundation for understanding women's representation, we contend that the existing research suffers from two limitations. First, the literature within political science and social movements tends to examine the participation of women in political institutions using discrete examples. Studies of participation examine either participation in the institutions of a single country or region (see, e.g,, Kittilson 2006; Norris 1985; Siaroff 2000) or the participation of women in a single institution across a number of countries (see, e.g., Caul 1999, 2001; McDonagh 2002). This approach leaves our understanding of women's participation in political life incomplete. While political science knows a great deal about women's participation in regions such as Latin America, we are at a loss to explain how those models of representation extend to other regions of the world.

Second, the existing literature tends to focus on specific forms of women's representation, such as the number of women in the legislature or the executive, without examining how representation in one form may impact representation in others. For us, the trends presented in Figure 1.1 raise an interesting question—are the across-the-board increases in women's representation interrelated? Put another way, we seek to understand whether women's legislative representation in any way explains the increases in women's representation in other areas. By simply examining the data, we can see that the general increase in women's legislative representation predates the increase in other areas of representation. However, there are no empirical studies that can definitively answer whether the increasing level of women's legislative representation explains, in part, the increases in other areas or whether the adoption of a quota or the election of a female executive affects women's representation in other areas.

This book attempts to answer these questions. Quite simply, we argue that women's representation in one area or institution does, in fact, affect women's representation in other areas. One major limitation of the existing literature is that there is no unifying theory to explain the variation we see across institutions, time, and region. While we ourselves have not found a completely satisfactory solution to this problem, we propose a theory that we believe pushes the field in this direction. We argue that, in order to understand the diversity of women's representation, one must consider the influence of women's participation in one democratic institution on another. We refer to this process as contagion. Using our dataset of 159 democratic countries for the years 1945–2006, we demonstrate that the level of women's representation in one institution impacts the level of women's representation in others. By using a dataset that covers democracies across the globe, we show that contagion is not simply an artifact of one region or country. While we highlight important regional differences, our research shows that contagion exists even when we control for these regional differences.

Explaining Women's Representation

Before adding our understanding of contagion, we must first examine the existing literature for the factors known to influence women's representation. We find several causal factors that determine the level of women's representation. The participation of women in public life, including the labor force, is a consistent influence on women's representation, giving women both the tools and the distinct preferences necessary for participation (Clark and Clark 1987; Escobar-Lemmon and Taylor-Robinson 2005; Hughes and Paxton 2008; Inglehart and Norris 2003, Jalalzai 2008; Norris 1985; Rule 1987; Salmond 2006; Siaroff 2000; Thames and Williams 2010; Williams and Thames 2008). Labor force participation is just one aspect of the overall level of development within a country that is positively related to greater participation by women (Htun and Jones 2002; Hughes and Paxton 2008; Jalalzai 2008; Matland and Studlar 1996; McDonagh 2002; Salmond 2006; Siaroff 2000; Vengroff, Nyiri, and Fugiero 2003). Labor force participation is also a function of women's increased educational opportunities and the availability of maternal leave and day care (Escobar-Lemmon and Taylor-Robinson 2005; Inglehart and Norris 2003), which are part of the explanation for the significant representation of women in public life in Scandinavian countries (Matland and Montgomery 2003; Matland and Studlar 1998). Of course, the extent to which a younger generation of citizens favors a different division of labor between the sexes can also influence the participation of women and their individual aspirations for office (Inglehart and Norris 2003; Wolbrecht and Campbell 2007).

It is not just women's participation in the labor force by itself that can influence women's representation in politics. Some professions may be more likely to produce female political aspirants than others (Lawless and Fox 2005; Matland 2006b; Matland and Studlar 1998; Williams 2008). The type of profession in which one works can influence a political candidate's ability to

gather resources for political office, including campaign donations and political connections that can be crucial to increasing the number of women
in office (Carroll 1994; Lawless and Fox 2005; Williams 2008). The extent to
which women participate in feeder occupations is an important consideration for studies of women's representation, as is the presence of women in
lower-level offices.

In thinking about the factors known to influence women's political participation, it is important to understand how these factors may vary over
time. Cultural shifts in support for the representation of women in politics,
for example, are an influence on women's representation, one that is best captured over time. Support for women's representation has been measured in
a number of ways, including surveys on support for female executives and
measures of the number of years since the first female was elected to office
(Hughes and Paxton 2008; Inglehart and Norris 2003; Jalalzai 2008; Salmond
2006; Thames and Williams 2010; Williams and Thames 2008). Past studies
include such measures to tap the support for women in office (the former)
as well as the extent to which there is a tradition of women's participation in
public life (the latter), both of which are manifestations of a culture supportive of women in office. If such factors were not examined over time, it would
be impossible to discern whether a threshold of support was necessary to
achieve women's representation and risk eliminating countries on the cusp
of producing female leaders—countries that could potentially enrich our understanding of representation if studied early enough.

In addition to the importance of support for women qua women, there
are other cultural factors worthy of exploration. Support for female candidates may increase with specific political conditions, especially the history
of corruption within a country (Baldez 2004; Escobar-Lemmon and Taylor-
Robinson 2005; Hughes and Paxton 2008; Jalalzai 2008; Paxton and Kunovich 2003; Valdini 2005). To the extent that women are viewed as political
outsiders, free of corruption, they may gather greater support for their candidacies within a country. Similarly, the ideology of the country and its emphasis on rights more generally also play a role in understanding representation, with left-leaning countries more likely to see women in power (Caul
1999; Hughes and Paxton 2008; Inglehart and Norris 2003; Jalalzai 2008;
Kenworthy and Malami 1999; McDonagh 2002; Siaroff 2000). Related to the
importance of ideology is the religiosity of a country, both in terms of the de-
nomination and frequency of attendance at religious services (Inglehart and
Norris 2003).

Differences in economic and cultural traditions certainly matter. Yet, previous research also clearly demonstrates that political institutions matter by

creating different incentives for political actors to foster women's representation. Electoral rules take many forms, including the differences between popular and appointive systems (Jalalzai 2008; Slotnick 1984); another influence is whether there are single-member or multimember districts (Caul 1999, 2001; Escobar-Lemmon and Taylor-Robinson 2005; Htun and Jones 2002; Hughes and Paxton 2008; Kenworthy and Malami 1999; Matland and Studlar 1996, 1998; McDonagh 2002; Norris 2004, 2006; Rincker n.d.; Salmond 2006; Siaroff 2000; and Vengroff, Nyiri, and Fugiero 2003). The greater the opportunities for parties to balance their ticket, the more successful women are at attaining political office. Higher district magnitude tends to favor greater representation by women (Darcy, Welch, and Clark 1994; Kenworthy and Malami 1999; Lakeman 1976; Matland 1993, 1998; Matland and Studlar 1996; Norris 1985; Reynolds 1999; Rule 1987; Salmond 2006; Thames and Williams 2010); in addition, more generally, the more seats up for election, the better women fare in elections (Matland and Studlar 1996; Welch and Studlar 1990). This is especially true for proportional-representation systems, where the advantages of incumbency are less important than in single-member systems (Matland 1993; Matland and Brown 1992; Studlar and McAllister 1991; Welch and Studlar 1996). The existence of a greater number of viable political parties increases the chances for women's participation (Matland and Studlar 1996), not only within left-wing parties that are more sympathetic to women, because the success of these parties encourages other parties to diversify to gain a larger percentage of the vote (Reynolds 1999).

A final factor that may influence women's representation within political institutions is the amount of power the institution and the individuals within it wield. There is some evidence that women are more likely to hold lower-level offices, which tend to be less powerful across the branches of government (Anasagasti and Wuiame 1999; Darcy, Welch, and Clark 1994; Hughes and Paxton 2008; Jalalzai 2008; Matland and Studlar 1998). To the extent that power is shared within an institution, such as in systems with both a president and a prime minister or on courts with a large number of judges, we should expect to see more women in power.

The Case for Contagion

Given the influence of so many factors on women's representation, one might wonder how contagion could improve upon what we already know. There are three main reasons why studying contagion may offer insight into our understanding of women's representation. The first, and most obvious, justification for considering contagion is that, as the group selecting members of the institution becomes more diverse, so should the institution. For example, in electoral systems where legislators are chosen through a proportional-representation list system, as the parties making the candidate list become more diverse, so should the legislature. Not only will there be more women with the political experience necessary to be an effective member of the legislature, but also more women within the party will push the party to put forward women for office or to adopt quotas (Baldez 2004; Caul 1999, 2001; Krook 2006a; Matland 2006b; Matland and Studlar 1996). Quotas can further increase the number of women in legislatures, creating an indirect contagion effect that diversifies other institutions. Similarly, as women gain political experience in the legislature, they become likely choices for cabinet-level positions (Escobar-Lemmon and Taylor-Robinson 2005; Jalalzai 2008; Siaroff 2000). The combined diversification of the legislature and cabinet should then also affect the representation of women on high courts, especially outside the United States, where judges are typically chosen by either one or both of these institutions (Williams and Thames 2008).

In addition to the influence of the diversity of the selector on the diversity of political institutions, contagion theory also suggests that as one political institution becomes more diverse, the perceived risk of diversifying other institutions is lessened. As leftist parties began putting female candidates forward or adopting quotas, other parties became increasingly likely to follow suit. Both the public and members of other political institutions saw that there were no negative consequences for diversifying, making them more willing to diversify themselves (Baldez 2004; Caul 2001; Krook 2006b; Matland 2006a; Matland and Studlar 1996). The larger the political institution (or the greater number of seats), the lower the risk of diversifying (Darcy, Welch, and Clark 1994; Lakeman 1976; Matland 1993, 1998; Salmond 2006). Thus, diversity in one institution should spill over into others, as political actors see few if any negative consequences for diversifying.

Finally, the diversification of one institution may influence diversity in another as institutions compete within a country for a finite amount of power. Past research demonstrates that more diverse institutions are seen as more legitimate by the masses, especially political minorities (Phillip 1995; Pitkin 1972; Schwindt-Bayer and Mishler 2005). As institutions attempt to advance their policy objectives, the legitimacy of the institution plays a key role in winning public support (Easton 1965, 1979; Norris 1997). Indeed, for institutions such as cabinets and the judiciary, which are not democratically elected, legitimacy may be crucial to winning adherence to their policies or decisions. Thus by bringing formerly unrepresented groups into the political fold, institutions not only gain an electoral edge but also gain advantage over other institutions as they move toward their policy goals. The ability to appeal to a wider swath of the electorate and the greater political efficacy people attach to more diverse institutions will make it easier for institutions in competition over the policy space to achieve their policy goals. This is especially important because these political minorities may view policy differently from those in the majority (Wenzel, Bowler, and Lanoue 2000).

The importance of understanding the influence of women's representation in one institution on other institutions is grounded in the importance of understanding representation generally. As more diverse interests are brought into the public domain, political minorities' ability to achieve new policy goals is dependent on the diffusion of political power across institutions. The link between descriptive and substantive representation can hardly be understated (see Catalano 2009; Kenney 2006; Razavi 2001; Sawer 2000; Schwindt-Bayer and Mishler 2005; Swers 2002). However, in most countries, it takes the work of more than one political institution to achieve these policy goals. The more diverse all political institutions are, the more support new policies will receive from these institutions, and the more likely these policy goals will be achieved.

The influence of contagion does not end with considering the number of women serving in other political institutions, however. These institutions become diverse because of the adoption of quota laws, both voluntary and compulsory. Quota laws are perhaps the single most important institutional mechanism affecting women's representation. The type of quota within a country can vary significantly, from reserved seats within an institution to targets where party compliance is either voluntary or mandatory, and can significantly influence women's representation, though the effect on women's representation may be unintentional (Anasagasti and Wuiame 1999; Baldez 2004; Caul 1999, 2001; Htun and Jones 2002; Hughes and Paxton 2008; Jalalzai 2008; Kittilson 2006; Krook 2006a, 2006b; Matland 2006a, 2006b; Norris 2004, 2006; Williams and Thames 2008). The greater the costs of noncompliance with quotas, the greater the impact the quota has on the number of women in office. The availability of sanctions for noncompliance with quotas is important because the real motivation for creating a target for women's presence may be not to increase the number of women within the institution but instead to gain an electoral advantage for the party without any real intention of compliance (Krook 2006a, 2006b). Thus, parties that prompt other parties to adopt quotas create a form of contagion (see, e.g., Caul 2001). Of course, the need for quotas within some institutions is still a matter of considerable debate and one about which women and men within the institution continue to have different views (Anasagasti and Wuiame 1999). Nonetheless, the indirect effect of quotas on diversifying institutions other than the parties or legislatures is worthy of consideration.

Other scholars have addressed contagion. Matland and Studlar (1996) argue that party leaders and even district-level constituency committees can feel pressure to nominate more female candidates as other political parties do so. There is also evidence that elites adopt gender quotas in response to decisions by other parties (Caul 2001; Meier 2004) or countries (Gray 2003; Powley 2005). Still other studies consider the influence of one institution on another (Escobar-Lemmon and Taylor-Robinson 2005; Jalalzai 2008). Yet, these studies tend to focus on contagion as a process that operates within one, narrow institution or form. We argue that contagion is much broader than diffusion through competition or regional proximity.

In this book, we focus on contagion from three sources—the level of women's legislative representation, the presence of a female chief executive, and the presence of gender quotas. As institutions such as the legislature or the executive become more diverse by the inclusion of women, we expect this diversity to impact women's representation in other areas. In addition, as individual parties or nations adopt quotas, we expect the commitment to gender equality to impact other institutions, as well. We test the impact of these contagion sources on women's legislative representation, the election of female chief executives, the selection of female judges to high courts, the adoption of voluntary party quotas, and the adoption of national quotas, both compulsory party quotas and reserved-seat quotas. If our contagion argument is correct, we expect these sources of contagion to impact women's representation in these areas.

Cases

For this project, we created a dataset with information on 159 democratic countries for the years 1945–2006. Table 1.1 lists the countries included in this analysis. They are all democracies, a function of two factors: democratic countries represented a substantial majority of all countries during this time period and offered women the greatest opportunity for political participation.[1] We used both Polity IV (2008) and Freedom House (2007) rankings to determine whether countries were democracies. We included all country years for those countries that achieved at least a score of six on the Polity2 variable from the Polity IV Project (2004) or were designated at least "partially free" by Freedom House (2007). While we begin each chapter with 159

Table 1.1. Countries in the Dataset

Albania	Ecuador	Malawi	Saint Vincent and
Algeria	Egypt	Malaysia	the Grenadines
Andorra	El Salvador	Maldives	Samoa
Angola	Estonia	Mali	San Marino
Antigua and Barbuda	Fiji	Malta	Sao Tome and
Argentina	Finland	Marshall Islands	Principe
Armenia	France	Martinique	Senegal
Australia	Gambia	Mauritania	Seychelles
Austria	Georgia	Mauritius	Sierra Leone
Bahamas	Germany	Mexico	Slovakia
Bangladesh	Ghana	Micronesia	Slovenia
Barbados	Greece	Moldova	Solomon Islands
Belgium	Grenada	Monaco	South Africa
Belize	Guam	Mongolia	Spain
Benin	Guatemala	Morocco	Sri Lanka
Bhutan	Guinea	Mozambique	Suriname
Bolivia	Guinea-Bissau	Myanmar	Swaziland
Bosnia and Herzegovina	Guyana	Namibia	Sweden
Botswana	Honduras	Nauru	Switzerland
Brazil	Hungary	Nepal	Taiwan
Bulgaria	Iceland	Netherlands	Tanzania
Burkina Faso	India	New Zealand	Thailand
Burundi	Indonesia	Nicaragua	Timor-Leste
Cambodia	Ireland	Niger	Togo
Cameroon	Israel	Nigeria	Tonga
Canada	Italy	Norway	Trinidad and Tobago
Cape Verde	Jamaica	Oman	Turkey
Central African Republic	Japan	Pakistan	Tuvalu
Chile	Kenya	Palau	Uganda
Colombia	Kiribati	Panama	Ukraine
Comoros	South Korea	Papua New Guinea	United Kingdom
Costa Rica	Latvia	Paraguay	United States
Cote D'Ivoire	Lebanon	Peru	Uruguay
Croatia	Lesotho	Philippines	Vanuatu
Cyprus	Liberia	Poland	Venezuela
Czech Republic	Liechtenstein	Portugal	Yugoslavia/Serbia
Denmark	Lithuania	Romania	and Montenegro
Djibouti	Luxembourg	Russian Federation	Zambia
Dominica	Macedonia	Saint Kitts and Nevis	Zimbabwe
Dominican Republic	Madagascar	Saint Lucia	

democracies, we lose observations due to missing data, lagged terms, and methodological differences across the chapters. The appendices list the cases used in each chapter.

We gathered information on representation in legislatures and quota law types from a number of sources (Caul 2001; Dahlerup 2005; Inter-

Parliamentary Union 2005, 2006; International Institute for Democracy and Electoral Assistance 2003, 2009; International Institute for Democracy and Electoral Assistance and Stockholm University 2006; Jones 2004; Kittilson 2006; Krook 2005, 2007b, 2009). Data on female executives were gathered from the Worldwide Guide to Women in Leadership (2009) and from Gleditsch and Chiozza (2009). Both the number of women serving on high courts and the characteristics of the court were gathered from court websites and through communication between the authors and the Ministries of Justice.

Given the lengthy time frame as well as the number of countries in our dataset, the best way to consider representation and the potential for contagion to explain representation is with a time-series, cross-sectional design (Hughes and Paxton 2008; Salmond 2006). The justification for the breadth of our project comes from the literature on women's representation itself. Past studies are replete with examples of how temporal and cross-national characteristics can serve to influence women's representation, while few examples consider both.

The importance of the design comes from the effects of time and space separately. The effect of time is the easiest to explain: women did not participate in politics in substantial numbers until the 1970s. Over time, however, the number of women in political institutions of all types has increased substantially (Hughes and Paxton 2008; Jalalzai 2008). In part, this is driven by two factors. First is the effect of term length and incumbency; the number of women in government at time (t) is a function of the number of women at time (t–1). Thus, we know that the number of women in political institutions at any point in time is a function of the number of women serving in years prior (Hughes and Paxton 2008; Jalalzai 2008). A second factor is the effect of descriptive representation; women serving in the past become role models for future female political aspirants (Lawless and Fox 2005; Wolbrecht and Campbell 2007). Unless there are women to break down the barriers of political institutions, women are less likely to run for office in the future (Carroll 1994; Hughes and Paxton 2008; Jalalzai 2008; Lawless and Fox 2005). Thus, looking at women's participation over time is an essential component of understanding women's representation.

Studying representation over time also allows us to better understand the effects of cross-national influences on women's representation. The literature on representation focuses on the influence of institutional rules, country demographics, and culture as explanations for the participation of women in public life. These cross-national factors known to influence women's representation may change over time within a country, affecting women's representation in a way cross-sectional studies alone are not able to capture. It is therefore important to consider each of these explanations both discretely within a particular year and over time. The literature on cross-national influences, as we note later, has begun to consider the importance of how these factors change over time and the influence of this on representation.

Chapter Outline

To understand contagion, as well as the other factors known to influence women's representation, we examine four areas: the legislature, the executive, the judiciary, and quotas, both party and national gender quotas. In chapter 2, we examine factors that explain women's representation in the legislature. The extant literature on women's participation tends to focus on the legislature, providing a rich grounding for our own work. We expect that women's legislative representation is at the heart of the contagion effect and will be strongly correlated with increased women's representation in other areas.

Chapter 3 focuses on those factors that explain the election of female chief executives. While some literature exists that examines women in cabinets, little work, to our knowledge, directly addresses women as chief executives (for exceptions, see Jalazai 2008 and McDonagh 2002). Using an original dataset of women chief executives, we show not only how social, cultural, and economic factors affect the likelihood of women being elected but also how women's representation in other institutions affects this likelihood.

In chapter 4, we examine the question of women's representation on courts. Courts are the last area where women have made inroads. The slow movement to the courts is often the result of a number of factors. First, many of these courts are new, so the opportunity for women to participate has been more limited historically. Second, the training and service requirements for those courts can limit women's access; women may not have had adequate experience in the public arena to win appointment. Finally, because the selection of judges typically requires the cooperation of two institutions, the need to diversify two bodies rather than one has slowed women's progress (Williams and Thames 2008). Nonetheless, we look at the role of women's participation outside the judiciary to understand the diversity on a country's high court.

We also analyze the adoption of both voluntary party quotas and national gender quotas. In chapter 5, we take on voluntary party quotas and show how the contagion effect can explain the adoption of these quotas. In chapter 6, we examine two types of national quotas—compulsory party quotas, which require parties to nominate a certain percentage of female candidates, and reserved-seat quotas, which designate a certain proportion of seats for female legislators. Here we examine how contagion impacts the adoption of both types. Moreover, we explore the differences in types of quotas and their adoption, an aspect of women's representation that has not yet been considered by the literature.

Finally, in chapter 7, we conclude by assessing the merits of our contagion argument. We present not only its successes but also its limitations. We also address the implications of our argument for the wider study of gender and representation.

Conclusion

Our project considers the variation in women's paths to participation in public institutions, where that path is open, where it is not, and what accounts for the differences in women's access. To that end, we consider the representation of women in political institutions over the past six decades, controlling for the factors that might affect representation within a single institution while also accounting for the contagion effect, or how the representation in one institution may influence another. The political institutions we consider include legislatures, cabinets, courts, and quota laws. By looking cross-nationally, cross-institutionally, and across time, we can gain a more complete perspective on women's representation. The breadth of this book offers a lot of opportunities for generalization, especially as countries consider alternate constitutional arrangements. As detailed later, the book explores the representation of women within institutions first and then builds to integrate a theoretical understanding of how women in one branch of government influence the representation of women in other institutions.

2
Understanding Women's Legislative Representation

In 1917, three years before the adoption of the 19th Amendment that prohibited voting restrictions based on gender, Jeannette Rankin of Montana became the first female member of the U.S House of Representatives. Two years later, in 1919, Viscountess Nancy Witchter Astor won a by-election to replace her husband as the Member of Parliament from Plymouth Sutton, becoming the first woman elected to the British House of Commons.[1] Two years later, in 1921, five women—Nelly Thüring, Agda Östlund, Elisabeth Tamm, Kerstin Hesselgren, and Bertha Wellin—were the first women elected to the Swedish parliament. Thus, in the span of only four years in the early twentieth century, three legislatures in well-established democracies all experienced something unfortunately very novel for the time—female legislative representation.

If we fast-forward to the twenty-first century, we can observe dramatic increases in the level of women's representation in many democratic legislatures. In 1945, the global average for women in democratic legislatures was slightly below 2 percent. By 2006, the average had increased significantly, to more than 17 percent. While certainly the average is significantly less than the percentage of women as a portion of the population, we have at least experienced significant increases in women's legislative representation since 1945.

The average of women's global legislative representation, however, masks significant variation among countries. While the Swedes failed to elect their first female legislators until four years after the United States, they did elect five to the Americans' one. In fact, the U.S Congress did not contain five female legislators until 1927. This Swedish "exceptionalism" continued into the twenty-first century. In 2006, more than 47 percent of Swedish parliamentary seats were held by women. In the United States, however, barely more than 16 percent of congressional seats were held by women. Among advanced, developed democracies, the United States was not the only laggard in terms of female legislative representation. In the United Kingdom, fewer than 20 percent of the seats in the House of Commons were held by women, while in the Japanese Diet fewer than 10 percent of seats were held by women. The United States, the United Kingdom, and Japan were surpassed not only by advanced, developed democracies such as Sweden, Norway, and Denmark but also by developing countries with shorter democratic histories, among them Grenada (26.7 percent), Mauritius (24.2 percent), Mozambique (34.8 percent), and Costa Rica (38.6 percent).

Explaining this variation has been a central point of emphasis for gender scholars. The work of these scholars has created a rich, dense set of theories to explain why some countries elect more female legislators than others. For some, the key difference is variation in culture (e.g., Bystydzienski 1995; Inglehart and Norris 2003; Norris 1987, 1993). Some cultures place a premium on equality and fairness, while others do not. Other studies focus on political factors such as female political mobilization (Matland 1998; Norris 1985; Rule 1987; Salmond 2006) or the ideology of political parties (e.g., Duverger 1955; Lakeman 1976; Studlar and McAllister 1991). The role of political institutions, in particular the electoral systems, frames the discourse of some scholars (e.g., Darcy, Welch, and Clark 1994; Kenworthy and Malami 1999; Lakeman 1976; Matland 1998; Matland and Studlar 1996; Norris 1985; Reynolds 1999; Rule 1987; Salmond 2006).

The existing literature forms an excellent foundation for our efforts; however, we add to this literature by focusing on how contagion impacts women's legislative representation. We build on the work of Caul (2001), Kittilson (2006), and Tripp and Kang (2008) to show how voluntary party quotas, compulsory party quotas, and reserved-seat quotas can dramatically increase women's representation. Thus, we provide strong evidence that contagion does, in fact, matter. Variation in contagion, therefore, is essential to understanding the global variation in women's legislative representation. Yet, we also see the limitations of contagion in this chapter, as well; we find, for example, that the presence of a female chief executive has no independent impact on the level of women's legislative representation.

The chapter proceeds as follows. First, we examine the patterns of women's representation between 1945 and 2006. Here we see the general increase in overall women's representation, as well as the significant variation in women's representation globally. We then review the existing literature on women's legislative representation, followed by an empirical analysis of representation. At this point, we present the results of our statistical models, which demonstrate the differences between the impact of short- and long-term factors on women's representation. We then turn to our analysis of the U.S case and show how institutional reform might affect women's representation there. In the conclusion, we explain the significance of our findings to our contagion argument.

Patterns of Women's Legislative Representation, 1945–2006

Legislatures are the primary institutions for popular representation in democratic countries. They are the central democratic institution through which individual voters affect policy outcomes. The electoral systems for choosing legislatures vary dramatically by country; therefore, patterns of legislative representation can vary. Some systems may enhance local representation over national, as do single-member district systems. Others may encourage more broad-based, national representation through high-district-magnitude proportional-representation systems. Regardless of the electoral system, voters elect legislators to represent their interests in policy making. There are often other elected political leaders in democratic systems; however, the legislature is the primary institution through which representation occurs.

Given the importance of legislatures to representation, it is not surprising that much attention is paid to women's legislative representation. How well are women represented in the world's legislatures? On the one hand, we have evidence that the global average percentage of women in legislatures has increased; on the other hand, this rising average obscures significant differences among countries. To show this variation, we created a dataset of 159 democratic countries between 1945 and 2006. We deliberately chose to create a dataset that includes as many countries from across the globe as possible.

While Figure 2.1 demonstrates an increasing global average for women in the legislature, it also reveals tremendous variation in the percentage of

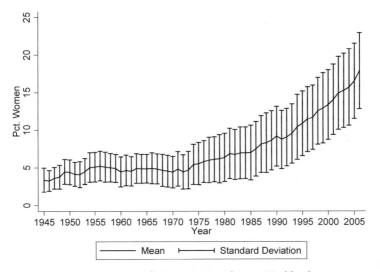

Fig. 2.1. Average Percentage of Women in Legislatures Worldwide, 1945–2006

women in the world's democratic legislatures. The standard deviation of the average is quite large in most years. Thus, we see significant differences among countries in terms of women's legislative representation. In 2006, women constituted 47.3 percent of Sweden's legislature; however, women constituted only 4.9 percent of the legislature in Sri Lanka. Two of the world's oldest democracies, the United Kingdom and the United States, elected legislatures in which women accounted for only 19.7 and 16.3 percent of the members, respectively. The variation among world legislatures clearly demonstrates that the increasing global average of women in the legislature is not characteristic of every country in our dataset.

Figure 2.2 plots the average percentage of women in the legislature by region of the world in our sample. Again, we see a general, upward trend in women's representation in all the world's regions between 1945 and 2006. Yet, we also see significant regional differences. Women's representation has consistently been greatest in Europe. For a brief period of time after the emergence of postcommunist democracies in 1990, Europe fell to second place behind North America. In 2006, the average for Central and South American countries equaled that for North American countries. The average percentage of women in legislatures in Africa, the Middle East, and Asia remains well below that of other regions, though it has increased significantly since 1945.

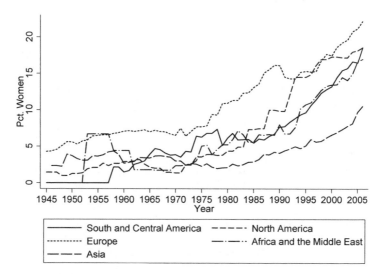

Fig. 2.2. Average Percentage of Women in Legislatures by Region, 1945–2006

This lack of proportionality raises a question about the fairness of the legislative process and the public policies it produces. The absence of proportional women's legislative representation becomes significant given the history of gender discrimination and inattention to core women's issues. Thus, increasing the number of women in the legislature is a critical issue. The presence of more women in a legislature, according to the logic, should increase attention to issues important to women. This argument, of course, is based on the assumption that fair representation of women's interests depends on the number of women in the legislature. The literature on women's substantive representation seeks to determine whether differences in gender lead to differences in representation. Some research on the United States finds that female legislators are more liberal than their male counterparts (Frankovic 1977; Leader 1977; Vega and Firestone 1995; Welch 1985). Yet, other research shows that these differences disappear once one controls for constituency (Barnello 1999; Burrell 1994; Schwindt-Bayer and Corbetta 2004; Simon and Palmer 2010). There is greater consensus around the idea that female legislators are more likely than their male counterparts to push for women's rights and to sponsor and pass legislation supporting women's issues (Berkman and O'Connor 1993; Bratton and Haynie 1999; Burrell 1994; Clark 1998; Dodson and Carroll 1991; Dolan 1997; Leader 1977; Norton 1999; Saint-German 1989; Swers 1998, 2002; Tatolovich and Schier 1993; Thomas 1994).

Outside the United States, studies of substantive representation have also produced mixed results. Some research points out that male and female legislators do not differ in their behavior other than in areas related to women's issues (Lovenduski and Norris 2003). The dearth of substantive representation in these cases may reflect the strength of party discipline (Celis 2008; Drewery and Brock 1983; Htun and Power 2006; Martinez-Hernandez and Euzondo 1997; Skjeie 1991). Put simply, female legislators may not have the power to represent women's interests because of the demands of party discipline. The ability of parties to limit the freedom of female (as well as male) legislators may vary by issue, the strength of the political party, and time, however (Cowley and Childs 2003; Dodson 2006; Sauger 2009; Shevchenko 2002; Wangnerud 2000; Wolbrecht 2002). The lack of consensus on women's substantive representation, if anything, highlights important differences between legislatures in terms of electoral systems, national experiences, history, and other factors. Celis (2008, p. 114) argues that "Context determines or at least influences the actors, acts and even the content involved in the substantive representation of women." The ability of women to represent women's interests directly is dependent on the context within which they operate.

One might argue that the absence of consistent evidence of substantive representation by female legislators renders the question of the number of women in the legislature moot. Simply increasing the percentage of women does not increase their substantive representation. Thus, the quality of women's representation is not dependent on the number of women. This argument, however, presumes that the impact of female legislative representation is determined solely by legislative or policy outputs. Descriptive representation—the degree to which a legislature's composition is similar to that of society generally—may also matter. Citizens may feel better represented simply by having a member of their group in the legislature. In the eyes of group members, the mere presence of one of their own may increase the legitimacy of the institution itself. One study of thirty-one democracies found that descriptive representation increased the responsiveness of the legislature to women's issues and increased its legitimacy (Schwindt-Bayer and Mishler 2005). The presence of strong, competitive female candidates increased adolescent girls' anticipated level of political involvement in one study of the United States (Campbell and Wolbrecht 2006). Another study of U.S. state elections found that the level of women's political engagement increased in the presence of "competitive and visible female candidates" (Atkeson 2003, p. 1040). This finding, however, is not universal even in the U.S. case (Lawless 2004).

The situation for aspiring female legislators has improved over the years in many countries; however, the data do suggest an uneven playing field. Research based on both substantive and descriptive representation suggests that the presence of women does matter. Thus, for individual women seeking legislative careers or for women more broadly who want better representation of their interests, the number of women in the legislature is an important question.

Explaining Women's Legislative Representation

Given the centrality of legislatures in policy making and popular representation, as well as the poor record of women's representation in many countries, it is no surprise that women's legislative representation is a central focus of gender research. Of great importance is the extent to which legislatures represent the interests of women. If male-dominated legislatures do not represent women adequately, the question becomes: Why are women underrepresented in freely, democratically elected legislatures?

For some, the key to explaining variation in women's legislative representation begins with recognizing that certain countries and regions tend to be associated with greater numbers of female legislators than others. The fact that women's representation is quite high in Scandinavian countries such as Sweden and Norway is the result of a well-known, strong cultural affinity for equality (Bystydzienski 1995; Norris 1987, 1993). In countries that lack this commitment to equality, women are more likely to be marginalized. Thus, there is thought to be a strong correlation between political culture and women's representation (Bystydzienski 1995; Inglehart and Norris 2003; Norris 1987, 1993). Societies with a deeper commitment to women's equality are more likely to elect women.

Key political differences among countries may also explain the variation in women's representation. One of the main factors often found to affect women's representation is the rate of women's participation in the labor force (Matland 1998; Norris 1985; Rule 1987; Salmond 2006). Women's participation in the labor force is thought to encourage women's political mobilization in at least two ways. First, as women enter the workforce in increasing numbers, they are more likely to become conscious of their political interests. Women exposed to discrimination are more likely to see the need to organize politically to prevent it. The more women become acquainted with other women in the workforce, the more likely they are to realize those political issues which they share. This type of consciousness raising is a precursor to political activity. Second, participation in the labor force makes political mobilization easier. Work may provide women with more resources, increasing their ability to organize. In addition, meeting other women in the labor force increases women's opportunities for finding other, like-minded women with whom to organize. Thus, female labor force participation serves as a proxy for women's political mobilization. The greater the level of women's political mobilization, the greater the support for women's candidates, which translates into greater women's legislative participation.[2]

The percentage of female legislators may depend on the ideological position of the parties that nominate candidates. For example, left-wing parties not only tend to be more supportive of women's issues but also are more likely to nominate female candidates. Consequently, several studies find that women receive more legislative seats as the support for left-wing parties increases (Duverger 1955; Lakeman 1976; Studlar and McAllister 1991). Thus, countries with stronger left-wing parties will maintain greater levels of women's legislative representation than those countries that feature softer support for the left.

Researchers have also tried to measure the impact of institutions on the level of women's representation. In particular, scholars cite the electoral system as an influential determinant of the number of female legislators. Such research consistently concludes that women's legislative representation is tied to the proportionality of the electoral system. More proportional systems produce greater levels of women's representation. More specifically, closed-list proportional-representation systems with greater district magnitudes tend to elect more women than do other types of electoral systems (Darcy, Welch, and Clark 1994; Kenworthy and Malami 1999; Lakeman 1976; Matland 1998; Matland and Studlar 1996; Norris 1985; Reynolds 1999; Rule 1987; Salmond 2006). Systems with low magnitudes, such as single-member district plurality systems, tend to discourage women's representation.

What explains the link between electoral systems and women's representation? Electoral proportionality increases as district magnitude increases, encouraging broader representation (Lijphart 1984). As Duverger (1954) first recognized, district magnitude is positively correlated with the number of political parties. Increasing the number of political parties creates greater opportunities for many parties, including left-wing parties that are more likely to represent women's issues (Matland and Studlar 1996). When there are more parties, electoral competition increases. This heightened competition creates pressure for parties to diversify their candidate lists in order to secure more votes (Reynolds 1999). Thus, adding women to the lists becomes a potential strategy by which to add votes.

The addition of female candidates poses fewer risks for parties in proportional-representation systems than it does for parties in other systems. The key here is that low-district-magnitude systems, such as single-member dis-trict plurality systems, create incentives for candidates to run on personal characteristics rather than party labels. Female candidates often face dis-advantages in these systems. Masculine personality traits are thought to be more important for politics than are feminine traits (Huddy and Terkildsen 1993). Thus, in elections based on personal characteristics, female candidates are disadvantaged. Research on U.S. Senate elections found a gender bias in media coverage that favored male candidates (Kahn 1992). Thames and Wil-liams (2010) demonstrate that electoral systems with strong personal vote incentives reduce the level of women's legislative representation more than other systems.

While systems with strong personal vote incentives may inhibit women's representation, more proportional systems, in particular closed-list systems, encourage women's representation. Scholars suggest several reasons for this. Matland (1998, pp. 112–113) writes that "female candidates must compete against existing interests within the party that are represented by men" in single-member district systems since parties can only nominate one can-didate per district. Yet, in systems with multimember districts, party lead-ers have the opportunity to create more diverse slates of candidates (Darcy, Welch, and Clark 1994; Lakeman 1976; Matland 1998; Salmond 2006). The cost of nominating female candidates is lower given that the party has the opportunity to select multiple candidates to satisfy multiple constituencies.

Proportional-representation systems also lack the strong incumbency advantages often found in majoritarian electoral systems. In systems with strong incentives for personal votes, candidates can create stable voting co-alitions based upon their personal characteristics, allowing them to win seats on a regular basis. Given this effect, turnover is lower, and female candidates face significant obstacles in overcoming entrenched incumbents (Matland and Brown 1992; Studlar and McAllister 1991; Welch and Studlar 1996). In-cumbents in closed-list systems do not enjoy this same level of influence. Since parties more directly control nominations, it is easier for party lead-ers to nominate female candidates rather than male incumbents. In fact, the weakness of incumbency advantages is one reason these systems tend to have a greater level of turnover, which strengthens the position of female candidates (Matland 1993).

Contagion and Women's Legislative Representation

Should we expect contagion to impact the level of women's legislative repre-sentation? The existing research highlights the impact of gender quotas on women's representation. Quotas can fall into three specific types: voluntary party quotas, compulsory part quotas, and reserved-seat quotas. Voluntary party quotas are by far the most common form of gender quota. They are adopted voluntarily by parties, meaning that they are not required by law. These quotas typically mandate that a specific percentage of legislative nominations go to women. Some include rules governing the placement of candidates on party lists. Compulsory party quotas require all parties in a country to reserve a certain percentage of their nominations for female candidates. These quotas are not voluntary; however, they may vary in their level of enforcement (Schwindt-Bayer 2009). Reserved-seat quotas are by far the rarest type of gender quota. These quotas reserve a specific number of legislative seats, not simply nominations, for female legislators. Existing research demonstrates that these quotas increase women's representation (Caul 2001; Kittilson 2006; Tripp and Kang 2008).

The existence of a female chief executive may impact female legislative representation, as well. Theories of descriptive representation argue that the presence of women in legislatures increases the institution's legitimacy and spurs women's political activism and engagement. It is possible that the presence of a female chief executive can similarly ignite sufficient political mobilization to increase women's legislative representation. Our review of the literature has not found research that tested this theory directly. However, given the literature on descriptive representation, it is possible that the presence of a female chief executive could spur the election of women to the legislature.

Analyzing of Female Legislative Representation in the World, 1945–2006

How well do these theories explain levels of women's legislative representation? To analyze the patterns of female legislative representation, we first undertake a statistical analysis of our dataset of 159 democratic countries between 1945 and 2006. In this analysis, we include only those years in which there was a legislative election. Thus, we remove those years for which there are no elections. This significantly reduces the number of observations in the data; however, given that the percentage of women in the legislature is very stable between election years, we were afraid that the inclusion of non-election years would significantly skew our results. Thus, we use only election years.

The data on women's percentage in the legislature pose several problems that directly impact the choice of our statistical model. First, the data are strongly autocorrelated, as discussed earlier.[3] To deal with this, we include the lagged value of the percentage of women in the legislature.

Second, it is highly likely that our data are heteroscedastic and that the errors are correlated with panels. In other words, our independent variables may not control for all attributes of individual countries (the panels) that explain the level of female representation. Thus, our model contains prediction errors. In addition, these errors are correlated across time, meaning that we may see a similar error for every electoral observation for a particular country. To deal with this, we fit Prais-Winsten regression models with panel-corrected standard errors. Thus, we are assuming that the errors are heteroscedastic and correlated across panels and corrected for these effects (Beck and Katz 1995).

Finally, our percentage women in legislatures dependent variable is "sticky," meaning that we see little change over time. Moreover, the change is often in only one direction—increasing. We conducted a Fisher unit-root test that found evidence of nonstationarity. The mean and variance of the percentage women in the legislature variable change over time. Associations we may find with nonstationary data may, in fact, be spurious ones; therefore, we follow Kittel and Winner (2005) and use the first-difference of the percentage women in the legislature in order to avoid this problem.

The factors that determine the level of women's representation may have both short- and long-term influences. Thus, we want to differentiate between the potential short-term, temporary effects of our variables and their long-term effects. To accomplish this, we employ a single-stage error correction model that contains lag terms for all variables and one period change (Δ) terms for all variables. The lagged terms measure the influence of our variables on the long-term equilibrium. The impact of variables in the long term depends on the magnitude of the change, the coefficient, and the extent to which the change continues over time, which itself is dependent upon the coefficient of the lagged dependent variable (Kaufman and Segura-Ubiergo 2001). Consequently, we measure the effect of the lagged variables by dividing their coefficients by the negative of the coefficient of the lagged dependent variable (Kaufman and Segura-Ubiergo 2001). The change terms measure the effect of short-term changes on women's representation. The coefficient of these variables represents the impact of a unit change in the independent variable on the dependent variable in one time period.

To model women's legislative representation, we use several independent variables designed to test the major theoretical arguments discussed previously. We include both the percentage of women in the labor force (Organization for Economic Cooperation and Development 2009; World Bank

2009) and the number of years since suffrage (Inter-Parliamentary Union 2008b). Countries with long histories of suffrage may be more culturally open to having women serve in office. In addition, we include labor force participation to measure political mobilization. Our dataset contains both developing and developed countries. Differences in levels of development may lead to variation in the percentage of women in the legislature, so we include the natural log of gross domestic product (GDP) per capita in constant 2000 U.S. dollars (World Bank 2009).

As Salmond (2006, p. 188) points out, controlling for political culture is complicated, since "the statistics simply are not available to directly measure political culture over a lengthy time frame." Both the years since suffrage and labor force participation are blunt instruments at best with which to account for culture. We include a series of regional dummies, which may pick up some of the cultural effects that are common to particular regions. Additionally, we include the percentage of women in the legislature lagged by one year to help control for culture and first-order autocorrelation.[4]

To control for electoral system effects, we include the natural log of district magnitude in all models (Beck et al. 2001; Golder 2005; Johnson and Wallack 2008). District magnitude is highly correlated with electoral system proportionality, so it is the best proxy for electoral system effects.

We include a dummy variable indicating whether in the country year there was a female chief executive. If contagion exists, we would expect that the existence of a female chief executive might spur the election of more female legislators. Other measures of contagion include our three variables for gender quotas. First, we include a dummy variable indicating the existence of a compulsory party quota. Second, we include a dummy variable indicating the existence of reserved seats for female legislators. We expect both of these variables to be strongly correlated with female representation. Finally, we include a variable that measures the number of parties in the election year with some form of voluntary candidate quota. We expect that, as the number of parties with quotas increases, so does the number of female legislators.

Last, we include a series of regional and decade dummy variables to control for time and space. We do not report the results of the decade dummy variables.

Table 2.1 presents the regression results of our models, using the change in the percentage of women in the legislature as the dependent variable. The results provide us with several interesting details. The first is that we have strong, consistent long-term effects for the majority of our independent variables on women's legislative representation. With the exception of the female in the executive variable, all other lagged variables are statistically significant

Table 2.1. Regression Results for Pct. Women in the Legislature

Independent Variable	Model 1	
	Coeff.	Std. Err.
Pct. Women $_{t-1}$	−0.147***	0.028
Natural Log GDP per Capita Constant U.S. $ $_{t-1}$	0.314**	0.157
Female Labor Force Participation $_{t-1}$	0.068***	0.014
Years since Suffrage $_{t-1}$	0.019***	0.007
Natural Log District Magnitude $_{t-1}$	0.531***	0.132
Female Executive in Year $_{t-1}$	−1.022	0.667
N Quota Parties $_{t-1}$	0.323*	0.183
Compulsory Party Quota $_{t-1}$	2.891***	0.78
Reserved Seat Quota $_{t-1}$	3.130**	1.279
ΔNatural Log GDP per Capita Constant U.S. $ $_{t-1}$	−3.598	4.755
ΔFemale Labor Force Participation $_{t-1}$	0.255**	0.112
ΔNatural Log District Magnitude $_{t-1}$	0.985	0.933
ΔFemale Executive in Year $_{t-1}$	−1.042	1.319
ΔN Quota Parties $_{t-1}$	0.751	0.536
ΔCompulsory Party Quota $_{t-1}$	−1.305	1.761
ΔReserved Seat Quota $_{t-1}$	5.848	2.406
South and Central America	−0.493	0.507
North America	−1.139	0.438
Asia	−0.806	0.386
Africa and Middle East	1.403	0.731
Constant	−4.866	1.652
Observations	510	
Countries	86	
R^2	0.205	
X^2	107.003***	

* p < 0.10, ** p < 0.05, *** p < 0.01

and positively correlated. A one-standard-deviation increase in the natural log of GDP per capita increases women's representation by 2.7 percent over the long term. If we increase female labor force participation by one standard deviation, we see a long-term increase of 5.9 percent in women's representation. The time since universal suffrage also positively impacts women's representation. A one-standard-deviation increase in years since suffrage increases women's representation in the long term, on average, by 2.8 percent.

The electoral system does matter even over the long run. A one-standard-deviation increase in the natural log of district magnitude increases women's representation by 4.6 percent. Thus, we find a substantive impact for the electoral system.

One of the most interesting findings presented here comes from the results of our lagged variables for party quotas. The results show that quotas of any type strongly impact women's representation. Increasing by one the number of parties with a voluntary quota increases women's representation by 2.2 percent, on average, in the long run. The substantive impact of a national quota, either a compulsory party quota or a reserved-seat quota, is quite strong. In the long term, a compulsory party quota and a reserved-seat quota increase women's representation by 19.6 and 21.2 percent, respectively. Thus, quotas have a significant, long-term positive effect on women's legislative representation, suggesting that contagion matters for women's representation.

The results also show that there are few short-term factors that improve women's legislative representation. Only two variables, the change in female labor force participation and the change in a reserved-seat quota, are statistically significant; however, both increase women's representation in the short term. A one-standard-deviation change in the female labor force participation change variable increases, on average, women's representation by 0.4 percent in the short run. The adoption of a reserved-seat quota increases women's representation, on average, by 5.8 percent in the short run. Given that reserved-seat quotas automatically reserve seats, not just the opportunity to compete for seats created by other quotas, this result is not surprising.

The results presented here clearly support much of the existing work. We find strong evidence that sociopolitical factors such as wealth, female labor force participation, and years since suffrage impact women's legislative representation. In addition, we find strong evidence that the electoral systems matter. We also find strong support for the positive benefit of some forms of contagion, especially all types of quotas. The adoption of quotas by parties or at the national level does increase women's representation.

Our regional dummy variables provide interesting results, as well. Two regions—North America and Asia—perform less well than our reference group, European countries. Both of these dummy variables are statistically significant and negatively correlated with women's representation. We do find that one region, Africa and the Middle East, performs better on average than Europe. The results clearly suggest that region does matter.

Discussion of Results

What is perhaps most interesting is that the influence of these variables apparently occurs primarily over the long run. Only two factors seem to instigate short-term changes in female legislative participation—changes in labor force participation and the adoption of a reserved-seat quota. The remaining variables achieve their impact only over the long run.

In terms of contagion, we found that quotas have a strong, positive long-run impact. Increasing the number of quota parties has a strong, long-run impact on the overall level of women's legislative representation. Thus, commitments by parties to gender equity do translate into real gains in women's legislative representation. We found that both measures of national quotas had a similar impact. Once again, we observe that quotas matter. In this case, a national commitment to gender equity via either a compulsory party quota or a reserved-seat quota increases the level of women's representation. We can conclude that contagion does matter.

There are limits to contagion, however. The presence of a female executive has no statistically significant impact on women's legislative representation. This may simply be a reflection of the relatively few women who have served as a chief executive. Yet, though it is statistically insignificant, we do see a negative correlation coefficient. In the end, we can conclude that the presence of a female executive does not create contagion in women's legislative representation.

Placing the United States in a Global Context

One of the advantages of undertaking our large-N statistical analysis is that it provides a framework through which we can place individual cases in a broader global context. By doing this, we can better understand why an individual country produces the level of women's representation that it does. One case that we believe is particularly interesting is that of the United States. If we compare women's legislative representation in the U.S. Congress with women's representation in the legislatures of the rest of the world, we find that the United States remains, at best, average and that in some eras it is below average.

Figure 2.3 presents trends for the United States, the world average, and the average representation of women in the legislatures of the pre-1974 members of the Organisation for Economic Cooperation and Development (OECD) excluding the United States between 1945 and 2006.[5] Only during a brief period in the 1990s did the United States exceed the world average for women's legislative representation. The U.S. record is well below that of the average pre-1974 OECD countries through this period of time. Thus, during this period, the United States remained a robust democracy on par with other countries, in particular the pre-1974 OECD, but it has consistently lagged behind other countries in terms of women's representation. We can conclude that the United States does not fare well in comparison with other advanced industrialized democracies.

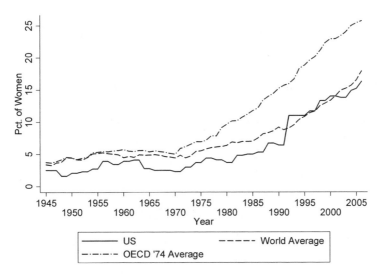

Fig. 2.3. Comparing U.S. and Global Women's Representation, 1945–2006

Why does the United States lag behind other advanced democracies? The robust literature on women's representation in the United States provides several explanations for the country's poor record. Research on the variation among American states finds evidence that states with more traditional political cultures tend to elect fewer women legislators to bodies at the state and the national levels (Arceneaux 2001; Burrell 1994; Nechemias 1987). Thus, states with more traditional political cultures, in particular those in the South, are less likely to elect women to Congress, depressing women's representation at the national level. Rule (1981), however, argued that the effect of culture was limited to only a few states. Prior to the 1980s, many of the states with traditional political cultures were dominated by the Democratic Party. Thus, historically, there was an association between support for the Democratic Party and weak women's representation (Nechemias 1987; Rule 1981). This effect, however, waned over time (Rule 1990).

To explain the limited number of women in the U.S. Congress, we need to determine whether there is something particular about American political culture that undermines women's representation and that does not operate in other countries. Existing research does not find that the U.S. political culture is dramatically different in terms of gender equality from the political culture of other countries. Using data from the World Value Survey, Hayes, McAllister, and Studlar (2000) show that feminist attitudes are less widely held in the United States than in some countries, such as Norway and Sweden, but more widely accepted there than some other countries, including Belgium, France, and Germany. Inglehart and Norris (2003) found lower levels of support in the United States than in Sweden for women as political leaders, but the level of support was similar to that in New Zealand, which has significantly more women in its parliament than does the U.S. Congress. Similarly, there is little evidence that the United States differs from other pre-1974 OECD countries in terms of gender inequality in the labor market (Tesch-Römer, Motel-Klingebiel, and Tomasik 2008). The increasing gender gap in voting behavior in which women voters are moving to the left and male voters are shifting to the right is found not only in the United States but also in other advanced industrial countries (Inglehart and Norris 2000). Thus, it is not obvious that differences in political culture explain the weak U.S. record on female legislative representation.

Another much debated topic focuses on differences in the levels of political ambition between men and women. Costantini (1990) found that women were less politically ambitious than men. Thus, the weak level of women's representation results, in part, from the fact that women are less interested than men in having political careers. Fox, Lawless, and Feeley (2001) argue, conversely, that women and men share equal levels of political ambition; however, women consider more factors than men do when deciding whether to run. Using a survey of state legislators, Fulton et al. (2006) concluded that women were less likely to seek seats in the U.S. Congress than men primarily because of their child-care responsibilities. However, this lower level of ambition does not translate into a weaker likelihood of standing for a seat. Weaker ambition is mitigated by greater responsiveness to the expected benefits of running for office. Yet, once in Congress, according to several scholars, women are less likely to run again (Lawless and Theriault 2004; Thomas, Herrick, and Braunstein 2002).

Again, if we were positing that women's lower level of ambition is the explanation for the U.S. record, we would need to know that women's ambition in the United States is less than in other countries. One of the problems is that scholars of Western Europe, for example, have traditionally blamed variation in women's representation on structural factors, not on differences in ambition (Davidson-Schmich 2006). One of the few studies of ambition in Germany found that, even with voluntary party quotas, a gender-based ambition gap remains (Davidson-Schmich 2008). More research needs to be done for us to understand fully whether significant differences in ambition exist between the United States and other countries; however, given the similarities in the political cultures of the United States and other countries, it is unlikely that such differences exist.

The U.S. research does highlight the role that electoral institutions play in undermining women's legislative representation. The weak level of women's representation is often blamed on the U.S. single-member district system, which presents obstacles to effective women's representation (Matland and Brown 1992; Rule 1981). As discussed earlier, high-district-magnitude systems with multimember districts are globally associated with greater levels of women's representation because they provide greater incentives for women's inclusion. One of the more common indictments of the U.S. system made by critics is that it creates strong incumbents and, therefore, reduces legislative turnover (Andersen and Thorson 1984; Welch and Studlar 1996; Zimmerman and Rule 1998). The advantages of incumbency create strong pressures for parties to avoid removing entrenched incumbents, most of whom are male, and replacing them with female candidates.

The fact that the U.S. electoral system creates strong personal vote incentives means that female candidates are less able than candidates in other systems to run campaigns based on party. Thus, it is no surprise that research on the United States also examines the effect of how gender attitudes, especially attitudes about gender roles, impact the election of women. In low-information campaigns, gender role attitudes are used as a proxy by voters (Alexander and Andersen 1993). Gender is used by some voters as a signal about their ideological orientations (Koch 2000). Fox and Oxley (2003) found that women are more likely to run for stereotypically female offices; gender, however, does not impact their likelihood of success. Thus, gender stereotypes impact the decision to run for particular offices but not necessarily the likelihood of success. Herrnson, Lay, and Stokes (2003, p. 244) found a somewhat different relationship between gender and electoral success. In their research, female candidates were more likely to win when they based their campaigns on issues that are stereotypically associated with women; in other words, they ran "as women."

Research on the U.S. case also highlights the interplay between gender and media coverage. Evidence at both the state and the national levels indicates that female candidates are often treated differently than men by the media (Kahn 199; Kahn and Goldenberg 1991). The media often portray female candidates in a more negative light than male candidates, which can undermine their voter support. The legislative gender gap is, therefore, spurred in part by differences in media coverage.

The literature on the U.S. case is interesting because so much of it leads squarely back to the electoral system. The negative effects of single-member district systems are noted in both the American and the broader comparative literatures. In particular, they both highlight how strong incumbency effects and weak legislative turnover create obstacles to women's representation. Moreover, two other explanations of the U.S. case—gender attitudes and media effects—may be salient in the U.S. case, given the nature of the electoral system. Both of these explanations rely on the fact that voters can easily identify and differentiate candidates on the basis of gender. In systems where parties are dominant and voters are asked to choose among parties, as opposed to candidates, this type of gender identification is surely less common. In the United States, however, the strong incentives for personal votes magnify the deleterious effects of gender stereotypes and media coverage because elections often turn on voters' perceptions of the individual candidates, rather than party.

The focus on electoral systems and their incentives found in the U.S. research is even more interesting if we compare the U.S. system to those in other OECD countries. Table 2.2 compares the averages of our key variables for the pre-1974 OECD countries in our dataset minus the U.S. data to the same averages for the United States alone. One of the most interesting differences is a result of the electoral system. The district magnitude for the United States, like all single-member district plurality systems, is one. All other OECD countries before 1974 had a district magnitude of 14.5. Other differences include these: the United States is wealthier, features a greater level of female labor force participation, and has a longer history of women's suffrage. Through our previous empirical analysis, we have determined that all three of these factors are correlated positively with women's representation. Thus, apart from district magnitude, it is difficult to explain the poor U.S. record by focusing on these explanations.

We found little evidence that district magnitude independently impacts women's representation in the long term; however, we did find a modest short-term impact. Given these results, it is difficult to simply associate the difference between the United States and other OCED countries on the basis of the limited, direct electoral system effects.

Yet, there remains one significant difference between the United States and many other pre-1974 OECD countries—gender quotas. No party in

Table 2.2. U.S. and Pre-1974 OECD Differences

Variable	Pre-1974	U.S.	Difference	P-Value
Avg. GDP Per Capita	$17,333.65	$25,018.72	$7,685.07	0.000
Avg. Female Labor Force	55.9%	60.2%	4.2%	0.032
Years Since Suffrage	44.4	48.9	6.5	0.019
Avg. District Magnitude	14.5	1	13.5	0.078

Note: P-values from a difference of means t-test

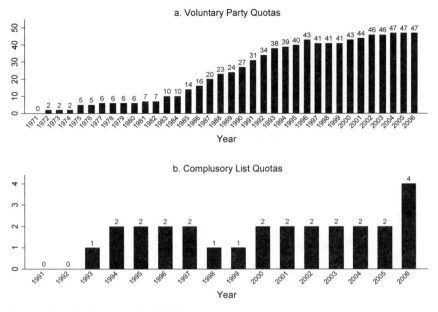

Fig. 2.4. Gender Quotas in the OECD

the United States uses a voluntary gender quota requiring that a minimum number of women be nominated for legislative seats. In addition, the United States has not adopted a compulsory party quota that compels parties to nominate a certain percentage of women. If we examine the pre-1974 OECD, we see a completely different picture. In 1972, two parties in the pre-1974 OECD adopted voluntary party quotas—the Liberal Party in Norway and the Liberal Party in Sweden. By 2006, as seen in Figure 2.4, forty-seven parties used voluntary party quotas. In 1993, Italy adopted a compulsory party quota, which was later declared unconstitutional; however, by 2006, four pre-1974 OECD countries employed compulsory quotas—Spain, Portugal, Belgium, and France.

Do differences in the electoral systems and the absence of quotas explain the relatively weak U.S. record on women's legislative representation? An answer to this question requires a counterfactual argument. We can at least attempt this by using our previous statistical models to simulate changes in the level of women's representation. Using the results from Table 2.1 Model 1, we calculate predicted changes in women's representation (Tomz, Wittenberg, and King 2003).[6] We present the results of three simulations. For all of them, we begin by setting all variables at their U.S. values in a given year. For the first simulation, we alter the values of the log of district magnitude and

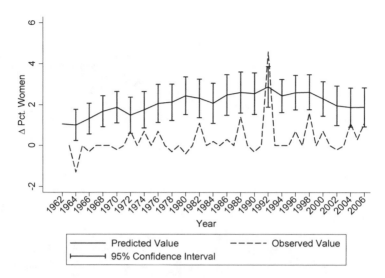

Fig. 2.5. Simulated U.S. Predicted Values with Increased District Magnitude

change of the log of district magnitude by setting them at the average of the non-U.S. pre-1974 OECD values. By doing this, we can simulate predicted values for the United States that reflect the impact of increasing district magnitude to pre-1974 OECD levels.

The results of this first simulation are presented in Figure 2.5. The figure presents two sets of trends. The first is the observed value of our dependent variable—the change in the percentage of women in the legislature. The second trend is the predicted change in the percentage of women based on our simulation. We also plot the 95 percent confidence interval around our simulated predicted values. If the observed value is outside or below the 95 percent confidence interval, we have a statistically significant difference between the observed value and the predicted value. Our predicted change is greater and statistically significant for nineteen of the twenty-two elections covered during this period. The observed change is greater than the predicted change in only one election—one in 1992, commonly called the Year of the Woman. The average yearly predicted change for the statistically significant predicted values is 2.2 percent. The observed yearly predicted change for these same elections is only 0.3 percent.

Figure 2.6 graphically presents the results of our second (top graph) and third (bottom graph) simulations. For our second simulation, we again set all values at their U.S. yearly levels. We then set the log of district magnitude, the change in district magnitude, the number of parties with quotas, and the change in the number of parties with quotas to their pre-1974 OECD levels. When we simulate the percentage change in women's representation in the U.S. Congress with the pre-1974 OECD levels of district magnitude and parties with voluntary quotas, we see a significant increase in the predicted values. The simulated predicted values are statistically distinct from the observed values for every election except for the 1992 election. For the predicted values, the year average increase was more than eight times greater —2.4 percent—than the observed yearly average, 0.3 percent.

Our final simulation attempts to measure the impact of the adoption of a compulsory party quota in the United States. Again, we set all variables at their yearly U.S. level except for the log of district magnitude, the change in the log of the district magnitude, the compulsory party quota variable, and the change in the national list quota variable. We simulate the adoption of a national list quota in the United States in 1992, the first year we observe a quota among pre-1974 OECD countries. The bottom graph in Figure 2.6 presents the results of this simulation. Again, with the exception of 1992, we find a statistically significant simulated change and a larger percentage simulated change than observed change. On average, the predicted change in women's representation is 3 percent, whereas the average observed change is 0.3 percent.

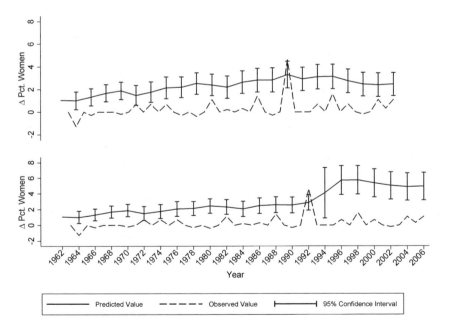

Fig. 2.6. Simulated U.S. Predicted Values with Gender Quotas

When examined in a global context, the United States has forces that should both spur and limit women's legislative representation. Its levels of women's labor force participation and wealth, both shown to boost women's representation, are greater than the average of its OECD counterparts. The United States granted full universal suffrage earlier than many of the other OECD countries, as well. Yet, the U.S. single-member district electoral system provides a significant hurdle to greater female representation. Not only does the broader comparative literature highlight how such systems undermine women's representation, but also research on the United States at both the national and the state levels similarly emphasizes the negative effects of the U.S. system on women's representation.

In addition, the United States lacks gender quotas. Currently, many nations in both the developed and developing worlds feature some sort of quota, whether voluntary party quotas, national candidate quotas, or even reserved-seat quotas. In the pre-1974 OECD countries, the spread of voluntary party quotas is clearly evident. By 2006, forty-seven parties had adopted some form of quota that required a greater percentage of female nominations for legislative seats. Only four countries adopted a national candidate quota by 2006; the United States has not followed this path, either. Our empirical results demonstrate that quotas of either type have significant positive impacts on women's representation globally. The fact that many countries in Europe and in Latin America, for example, have such quotas explains, in part, why they have stronger records of women's representation than the United States.

Our simulations illustrate the potential positive impact that electoral system reform and the adoption of some sort of gender quota might have on women's representation in the United States. In all simulations, we found strong evidence that the percentage of women in the U.S. Congress would significantly increase if the United States were to adopt one or all of these features. The fact that the United States has not followed the path of other countries should not minimize the important improvements we have seen in women's representation in the United States. Yet, it does highlight the impact that institutions have on women's representation, even when controlling for other cultural and socioeconomic factors. In addition, it raises the question of what factors lead to the adoption of these institutions. Electoral systems are resistant to change by their nature, and significant electoral reform is a relatively rare event. However, the adoption of gender quotas seems to be a more common and recent phenomenon. Thus, if we are to understand why the United States remains behind other nations in terms of representation, it is important to understand the impact of culture, socioeconomic forces, and the electoral system and also the reasons the United States has not adopted gender quotas, which seem to be increasingly common in other systems.

Conclusion

Globally, we have witnessed significant increases in the number of women holding national legislative seats. Yet, this global trend obscures real differences among countries. Our statistical analysis sought to explain this variation by testing arguments found in the existing literature on women's representation. In addition, we add to this rich literature by distinguishing between the short- and long-term effects of critical variables. Our results overwhelmingly show that those factors that increase women's representation operate over the long term. Key socioeconomic factors such as wealth and female labor force participation impact women's representation over the long term. We also find that, over the long term, increases in the number of years since universal suffrage increase the number of female legislators. Institutions also matter in the long term. While we find that the electoral system and the number of parties with voluntary quotas have no long-term effect, we also find that both compulsory party quotas and reserved-seat quotas have a strong impact on women's representation. We find evidence that short-term factors impact women's representation, as well. Changes in the electoral system, the level of female labor force participation, and the adoption of a reserved-seat quota all impact women's representation.

Our analysis of the U.S. case uncovers those factors that explain why the rate of women's representation in the United States lags behind the rate in other advanced, industrial democracies. The research on women's representation highlights the electoral system as a significant culprit in creating the weak U.S. record. Our simulations show that changing the electoral system would lead to an increase in the number of women in the U.S. Congress. We further demonstrate the potential impact of the adoption of voluntary party quotas and compulsory party quotas on U.S. women's legislative representation. The adoption of quotas, which are increasingly common in many OECD countries, would significantly increase women's representation in the U.S. Congress.

What about contagion? We find mixed evidence on the question of whether variations in women's representation outside the legislature can explain variations in women's legislative representation. On one hand, we found strong evidence that contagion in the form of both national quotas and voluntary party quotas can increase women's legislative representation.

The desire to increase gender equity through the adoption of quotas positively impacts the level of women's legislative representation. Thus, a commitment to improving women's representation in one area impacts directly women's representation in another. This is in line with our expectations based on our contagion argument.

On the other hand, we also find limits on contagion. We find little evidence that the election of a female executive impacts women's legislative representation. Thus, the variation in women's executive representation cannot explain the variation in women's legislative representation. What explains this finding? It may be an artifact of the relative scarcity of female executives. Not only are there few female chief executives, but also they are a fairly recent phenomenon. Over time, as we see greater executive gender diversity, we can expect diversity in this area to increase diversity in other areas and institutions, including the legislature. As of yet, however, we do not find such an impact.

3
Women and the Executive

Women's participation in executive office is perhaps one of the most misleading areas to study in women's political life. High-profile cases of female prime ministers and presidents seem to date back fairly far, with the first female prime minister serving as long ago as 1960. Moreover, the women serving in these high-profile positions are well-known politicians, including Indira Gandhi, Golda Meir, Margaret Thatcher, and Angela Merkel. While these high-profile and, in some cases, long-standing examples immediately come to mind when we think about women's participation in executive office, the idiosyncratic nature of the examples masks the real story of women's representation. Women's political participation in executive office is really a story of repeated examples, where women are elected more than once in some countries and none at all are elected in others. In fact, women served as the executive of the country in a mere 3 percent of the 159 democracies represented in our database covering the years 1945–2006, and more than half of these women served in the position on an interim basis.

Yet, even within this pattern, we find strong evidence of contagious representation. We find that, while the percentage of women in the legislature has an effect on both the probability of a female executive and the time to a country having a female executive, quota laws are related to representation, as well. This effect is consistent with our other findings throughout this book. Increasing women's political representation in the legislature and adopting quota laws both have a positive effect on women's representation as national executives. Thus, our analysis of female chief executives strongly supports our contagion argument.

This chapter begins with an exploration of the conditions leading to women's first attaining executive office and then examines how these conditions have varied over time. By first exploring what conditions led to women's participation in executive office as well as how time affected these factors, we can establish a more complete explanation of women's representation. Moreover, we can begin to predict what conditions will lead to the selection of women executives in the future.

Explaining Female Executives

Studies of women in executive office are relatively uncommon in the literature on women's political representation, likely because of the dearth of women serving in such office. The few studies that have considered female executives offer a useful starting point for this analysis, but we are able to go further. Instead of truncating our sample to predict participation in the modern era (Jalalzai 2008), describing the first female executive from the point of her election (Genovese 1993; Opfell 1993), or focusing on the cabinets (Adams and Scherpereel 2010; Davis 1997; Escobar-Lemmon and Taylor-Robinson 2005; Hult 2007) we take a different view. Consistent with other gender scholars (see, e.g., Paxton and Hughes 2008), we argue that it is important to understand the dynamics of time and how they affect women serving in executive office. This may be especially important for understanding women in executive office; some countries have repeatedly chosen female executives, while others have not. We can assess to what extent past participation by women in the executive and other offices affects future participation. Moreover, modeling the nonevents shows just how rare women's representation in executive office is. The rarity of the event requires a different statistical approach than that used in past studies. A focus on the modern era or on a few key cases leaves out the question of what country conditions are necessary to get a woman in executive office—in other words, what conditions are conducive to women's political participation. Finally, because of the breadth of our time period and data, we can explore the extent to which women's participation in the legislature spills over into women in the executive.

The factors known to affect women's political representation are drawn largely, though not exclusively, from studies of legislative office. After considering the more general factors known to affect women's political participation, we turn to an exploration of the elements of executive office that, in addition to having an independent effect on women's representation, alter the effects of the variables known to influence women's participation.

The existing literature on women's representation focuses on both supply- and demand-side factors (Matland 1993; Norris 1997). Supply-side factors are elements of the individual, including social background, resources, and ambition to hold office. While the characteristics of the individual are interesting, they are outside the bounds of our cross-national work. Studies that examine women's representation in office at the country level focus more on the effect of demand-side influences on women's representation.

Demand-side influences include socioeconomic, cultural, and institutional factors that may influence women's political participation. Among the socioeconomic factors that affect women's representation, a country's level of development is essential to women's representation (Davis 1997; Escobar-Lemmon and Taylor-Robinson 2005; Inglehart and Norris 2003; Jalalzai 2004, 2008; Matland 1998; Norris 1997; Paxton and Hughes 2008). While many thought that the level of development of a country had a linear relationship with representation, Matland (1998) was one of the first to consider the possibility of a nonlinear relationship, finding that less-developed nations did not follow the same patterns as more developed nations. In the developed world, countries with higher GDPs were more likely to see women participating in politics, whereas GDP was not a predictor in less-developed countries.

In addition to development, women's access to education and the labor force also influences their representation in political office, though the effects for cabinet positions are somewhat mixed (Adams and Scherpereel 2010; Escobar-Lemmon and Taylor-Robinson 2005). Typically, as women enjoy expanded access to education and participate more in the labor force, they develop both the skills necessary to participate in political life and the political connections necessary to campaign effectively (Adams and Scherpereel 2010; Carroll 1994; Davis 1997; Duerst-Lahti 2007; Escobar-Lemmon and Taylor-Robinson 2005; Inglehart and Norris 2003; Jalalzai 2004, 2008; Lawless and Fox 2005; Matland 1998; Norris 1997; Paxton and Hughes 2008). While education and labor force participation factors work hand in hand with development, they also exhibit an independent effect on women's representation.

Cultural factors also play a role in women's political participation. To the extent that the citizens of a country are open to women's participation in politics, women are more likely to participate or at least to campaign for such office (Duerst-Lahti 2007; Falk and Jamieson 2003; Heldeman 2007; Inglehart and Norris 2003; Kennedy 2007; Farrar-Myers 2003, 2007; Thomas and Schroedel 2007). This is especially important for the individualized offices of the executive (Jalalzai 2008). Unfortunately, data from measures of openness to women executives, such as the Gender Equality Index and other measures of public attitudes, are often available only from advanced countries and cover recent years. Other variables, however, may tap into a similar concept. For example, a number of studies consider the tradition of women's participation within a country (Inglehart and Norris 2003; Jalalzai 2008; Thames and Williams 2010; Williams and Thames 2008). Countries with a greater tradition of women's political participation, as measured by the number of years since suffrage was granted, typically see greater participation by women in office, and we should expect the same for executive office.

One cultural factor that may prompt changes in attitudes to women's participation is international pressure. Escobar-Lemmon and Taylor-Robinson (2005), for example, explored the possibility that the Beijing Protocol of 1995 had an impact on the recruitment of women for public office, drawing the attention of the international community to those countries where women were underrepresented in public life. More generally, a global focus on women's participation in public life may serve to bring more women into the fold.

A final set of characteristics known to affect women's participation in office comes from the political context, including women's opportunities to enter political life. Women's political organizations can be important in recruiting women for public office (Burrell 2006; Clift and Brazaitis 2000; Costain 2003; Davis 1997), though few countries have such institutions. More entrenched institutions that can influence women's participation include political parties themselves (Burrell 2006; Conroy 2007; Haussman 2003). Leftist parties are often important in increasing the number of women in office, including the development of quotas (Caul 2001; Htun and Jones 2002; Krook 2009).

Other factors that affect the political opportunity structure include the professionalization of and competitiveness for the office in question (Carroll 1994; Lawless and Fox 2005; Matland and Studlar 1998; McDonagh 2002; Sanbonmatsu 2006; Schwindt-Bayer and Mishler 2005; Vengroff, Nyiri, and Fugerio 2003). More professionalized offices are less likely to be filled by women. Similarly, fewer women seek offices for which elections are more competitive, with increased competition diminishing women's chances (see, e.g., Lawless and Fox 2005).

The professionalization and competitiveness of the office are in part a function of the power of the office, which is not the case for legislatures. In fact, there are a number of characteristics of executive office that may alter what we know from existing studies of women's representation. To begin, executive offices offer substantially fewer opportunities for women's participation than any other political institution. Unlike legislatures, national courts, and even ministerial positions, countries have at best two positions available for the executive and typically only one. Thus, to the extent that competition decreases women's odds of holding office, we should expect there to be relatively few female executives. While this news is not earth-shattering, it does mean that modeling representation of women executives is modeling an unlikely occurrence.

Not only is there more competition for fewer seats with executive office, but the types of office are unique to the institution. Presidential and prime minister positions differ substantially from other offices, in part, because they are a unified source of power, while legislators and judges share power. Even in systems where there is both a president and a prime minister, the shared power is divided between two people, creating more opportunity to exercise individual initiative than exists in other political offices. Not surprisingly, then, women are more likely to serve in one of these executive offices when there is a shared power structure, but their participation is still unlikely overall (Jalalzai 2008).

Related to the power differences of executive office is the importance of interim office holders. Much like the widow effect (Solowiej and Brunell 2003) in legislative offices, a substantial number of the women holding executive office were replacing husbands or fathers, who for a number of reasons were no longer the country's executive (Genovese 1993; Jalalzai 2004; Opfell 1993). In part, these women came to office to fulfill the agenda of their relative, making them a less radical choice for executive than if they had been elected in their own right. In fact, part of the argument in favor of these women is that their move to executive office was *not* radical; these women were carrying on the work of someone else. Having a woman holding executive office was meant to quell political unrest, not to represent large-scale change. Thus, the circumstances that lead to non-interim female executives should be different from those we find in the model of all female executives.

One final aspect of executive office to consider is the variation in the selection of executive offices. The ties of the prime minister and of an independently elected president to the legislature deserve closer scrutiny. First, access to the prime ministerial post is controlled exclusively by the party, making party service and party quotas incredibly important for women hoping to

achieve executive office; this also reduces the total number of eligible candidates for the office. The existence of a clearly defined pool of candidates,
along with a clear set of criteria for the office, not only makes women more
likely to hold this office but should also increase women's interest in the office (Davis 1997; Jalalzai 2004, 2008).

Further reinforcing the differences between presidents and prime ministers are the paths to office. The need to campaign in a national election is more
likely to reduce women's participation than is the requirement for party service that results in positions as prime minister. Not only are women less likely
to have the resources to launch a national campaign; they also dislike the act
of campaigning for any office, especially in the United States (Duerst-Lahti
2007; Lawless and Fox 2005; Farrar-Myers 2003, 2007; Williams 2008). These
differences between presidents and prime ministers should result in fewer
women holding executive office in presidential systems than in proportional-
representation systems, all else being equal (Jalalzai 2004, 2008).

It is because of the differences in types of executive that it is so important
to include elements of contagion. Prime ministers are chosen from the legislature, meaning that, as the percentage of women in the legislature goes up,
the odds of selecting a female prime minister should also increase. While
some studies have considered the influence of legislative representation on
executive representation (Jalalzai 2008; see Adams Scherpereel 2010 and
Escobar-Lemmon and Taylor-Robinson 2005 for cabinet examples), we are
able to go further, testing the variation over time.

Moreover, one would expect that the presence of a quota law should influence the likelihood of a female executive. Both national reserved-seat and
compulsory party quotas, while often more about women's access to the
ballot and the legislature, can also have an indirect effect on other political
institutions (see Williams and Thames 2008). Quotas not only increase the
number of women serving in the legislature but also raise awareness about
women's political participation more generally. The higher the number of
parties with voluntary quotas, the more likely the selection of a female executive. Thus, we should expect countries with quota laws, both voluntary
and compulsory, to be more likely to have female executives.

Data and Methods

In order to understand the factors that affect women's participation as national executives, we examined women's participation in executive office
using our database of women's representation from 1945 through 2006 in 159
democracies, with country year as the unit of analysis. During this period,

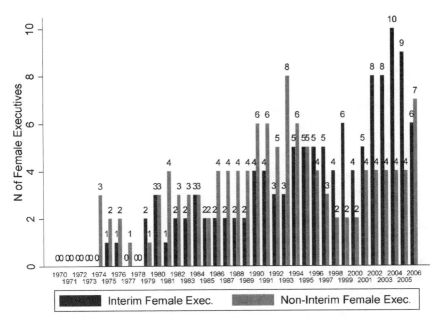

Fig. 3.1. Female Executives over Time

there were 279 instances where a woman was serving as executive of the country in that year, including women who served as interim executives. The number of countries, however, with a female executive is much smaller.

Figure 3.1 shows the increase in the number of countries with female executives during this period. Not surprisingly, substantially fewer countries have had non-interim female executives. Interim positions, however, should not be discounted. These positions are one of the first ways women gain executive office (Jalalzai 2004) and can perhaps allay concerns about women's ability to hold executive office. Nonetheless, the analysis must account for the differences in the initial office held.

To predict the factors that affect women's political participation during this period, we include variables for parliamentary systems, women's participation in the labor force, women's representation in parliament, the number of years since women were granted the right to vote, the natural log of GDP per capita in constant U.S. dollars, and whether or not the country has a reserved-seat or compulsory party quota law in effect. Additionally, we include a count of the number of parties within the country that have voluntary quotas. We also include decade dummy variables to account for the increasing awareness of women's political participation over time (results not shown), and regional controls to account for variation in women's political participation. The factors account for the demand-side influences discussed earlier, including women's opportunities for participation, culture, development, and the key variable—contagion. Women's participation in executive office is correlated both with percentage of women in the legislature and with the presence of quotas in the country, suggesting that contagion is a factor that affects women's participation in executive office.

Findings

The first models we estimate are multilevel mixed logit models that predict the instance of a female executive in each country year. A multilevel mixed logit allows us to calculate both fixed and random effects. We calculate random effects for each region and fixed effects for the remaining variables. For both of our models, we present the results of a likelihood-ratio test (L.R.) that compares the result of the mixed model with our random effects with a typical logit model without random effects. Both tests are statistically significant, meaning that the inclusion of random effects for regions is justified. We separate out women serving as a non-interim executive from a model with all female executives to see whether different factors affect the likelihood of a woman getting elected on her own.

Table 3.1 presents the results of our multivariate models predicting female executives. Model 1 shows the results for any instance of a female executive,

Table 3.1. Predicting Female Executives

Independent Variables	Model 1		Model 2	
	Any Female Exec. Coeff.	Std. Error	Non-Interim Female Exec. Coeff.	Std. Error
Parliamentary System	0.435*	0.223	0.857**	0.335
Pct. Women$_{t-1}$	0.063***	0.013	0.100***	0.019
Years since Suffrage	0.020***	0.005	0.018**	0.007
Female Labor Force Part.	−0.018**	0.007	−0.015	0.01
Log of GDP per Capita	−0.418***	0.086	−0.591***	0.122
Compulsory Party Quota	−0.693	0.538	−0.947	1.04
Reserved Seat Quota	1.147**	0.492	1.922***	0.557
N Quota parties	−0.164*	0.086	0.054	0.123
Constant	−2.616**	1.133	−1.836	1.529
Region (Variance)	0.792	0.578	1.041	0.805
Observations	2347		2347	
Countries	114		114	
Wald X^2	96.10***		86.15***	
L.R. X^2	43.65***		36.28***	

* p < 0.10, ** p < 0.05, *** p < 0.01

Table 3.2. Values of Regional Random Effects, Models 1 and 2

Region	Random Effect Model 1	Random Effect Model 2
South and Central America	−1.097	−1.206
North America	−0.087	0.402
Europe	0.868	−0.166
Africa and Middle East	−0.501	−0.262
Asia	0.989	1.505

while Model 2 shows the results for non-interim female executives. The results indicate that some variables consistently predict across both models, while others are significant in only one of the two. Parliamentary systems, percentage of women in the legislature, years since suffrage, the natural log of GDP per capita in constant U.S. dollars, and reserved-seat quotas, for example, all predict across both models. Female labor force participation and the number of parties with voluntary quotas are significant only in Model 1. Female labor force participation and logged GDP per capita are signed negatively, counter to the literature, but all other variables are in the expected direction. To understand the impact of the region, we estimated random effects for the regional variables.

The results show that region is significantly related to female executives. Model 1 shows that European and Asian countries are more likely to have a female executive, all else being equal. Model 2 shows that non-interim executives are more likely in North America and in Asia. To interpret the effect of the substantive variables, we estimated predicted probabilities . The results are discussed later.

The baseline probability of a female executive in Model 1 is 0.8 percent. This baseline was calculated by holding all continuous variables at the mean and all dichotomous variables at the mode. Substantively, this baseline is a parliamentary democracy in Europe before 1980, with 8 percent of legislative seats held by women, in which women were granted the right to vote more than thirty-four years prior, with a logged GDP per capita of 8, no quota law, 0.5 quota parties, and approximately 55 percent of the labor force female. Shifting from a parliamentary to a nonparliamentary regime reduces the probability of a female executive by 0.3 percent. With an increase of one standard deviation in the percentage of women in the legislature, the probability of a female executive rises to 1 percent, and a decrease of one standard deviation in the percentage of female legislators drops the probability of a female executive to 0.5 percent. Years since suffrage has a similar effect, with an increase of one standard deviation in the years since suffrage raising the probability of a female executive to 1 percent. Decreasing the number of years since suffrage by one standard deviation lowers the probability of a female executive to 0.6 percent. Female labor force participation and logged GDP suggest the same effect of diminishing returns. Because the mean for female labor force participation is so high, increases in the value of the variable decrease the likelihood of a female executive. The same is true for GDP.

The variables measuring the effect of quotas show some interesting results. Increasing the number of quota parties by one standard deviation decreases the probability by 0.1 percent. Yet, decreasing the number by one standard deviation increases the probability by 0.1 percent. Countries with reserved-seat quotas are more than three times as likely to have a female executive overall. These results suggest a significant impact for contagion on women serving as executive.

The predictions for non-interim female executives in Model 2 resemble somewhat those for Model 1. The baseline prediction finds that there is a 1 percent probability of a non-interim female executive. Changing from a parliamentary to a nonparliamentary system decreases the probability of a female non-interim executive by 0.8 percent. An increase of one standard deviation in the percentage of female legislators raises the probability to 3 percent, while a decrease of one standard deviation lowers the probability to less than 1 percent. Increasing the number of years since women were granted the right to vote increases the probability of a non-interim female executive to 2 percent, while an increase of one standard deviation in the years since suffrage decreases the probability to less than 1 percent. Once again, wealthier countries and those with a significant number of women in the labor force are less likely to have women serving in the executive, all else being equal. The impact of quota laws is even greater. Countries with reserved-seat quotas are eight times more likely to have a female executive than those without the quota law.

The significance of the percentage of the legislature that is female and the years since suffrage require more explanation to understand the substantive significance of these variables. Using the same baseline discussed earlier, we estimated the impact of each variable over a much larger range in Figures 3.2 and 3.3. The charts, however, estimate predictions beyond the range of our data and are meant to show at what point in each variable the probability of a female executive (any type) approaches 50/50.

Perhaps the most important conclusion to reach from these charts is that the likelihood of a female executive does not reach 50/50 until at least 60 percent of the legislature is female. Years since suffrage alone, however, cannot significantly increase the probability of a female executive. While these two variables have by far the greatest substantive significance on female executive, these factors alone cannot help women attain executive office.

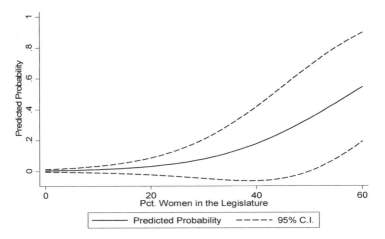

Fig. 3.2. Probability of a Female Executive by Women in Legislature

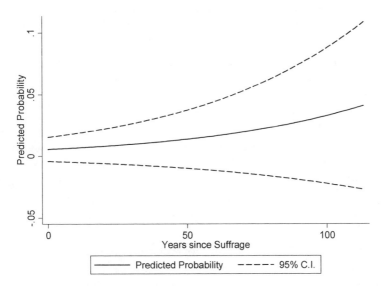

Fig. 3.3. Probability of a Female Executive by Years since Suffrage

Time to a Female Executive

Another way to think about the conditions necessary for women to gain executive office is to use duration models to determine at what point a country's conditions are ripe for a female executive. This approach is different from the previous models because we are measuring the time to an event, not just the event itself (Box-Steffensmeier and Jones 1997, 2004). The factors used to predict the time to an event are not different from those used earlier, so no additional explanation of the variables is necessary, though we did collapse the quota variables into a single measure to provide more variation and excluded the number of parties with quotas. Some discussion of the type of duration model, on the other hand, is necessary.

The move to duration models changes the dependent variable from whether or not a country elected a female executive to when. Duration models are increasingly common in political science (see, e.g., Box-Steffensmeier 1996; Box-Steffensmeier and Jones 1997, 2004; Box-Steffensmeier and Zorn 2001; Hettinger and Zorn 2005; Meinke 2005, to name just a few examples). These models are particularly helpful when data are censored and there are variables whose impact changes by time (also called time-varying covariates). Both of these features are present in our data. The models in this chapter are predicting the election of a female executive from the time the country enters our data as a democracy until it leaves our data, either in 2006, at the end of the dataset, or because it is no longer a democracy. The dependent variable is a country's survival time, measuring the time to the presence of a female executive. The dependent variable has the potential to be a repeated event.

The choice within types of duration models depends on the structure of the data. If we expected that the impact of our variables would be constant over time, we could estimate one of the proportional models such as exponential, Weibull, or Cox proportional-hazards models. Some of these models are more flexible than others, with exponential and Weibull setting a specific distribution, while the Cox proportional-hazard model does not require specification of a particular form but does require proportionality of the entire time period (Box-Steffensmeier and Jones 2004). For our purposes here, we cannot assume proportionality. A graph of the survival function over time clearly indicates that proportionality is violated (the step pattern is not consistent over analysis time). As we move forward in time, variables such as GDP, percentage of women in the legislature, and female labor force participation change values within a country, making them time varying covariates.[1]

By setting a number of the variables as time-varying covariates we can incorporate the dynamics of factors such as the percentage of women in the legislature into the model. In doing so, we can determine whether the change in the percentage of women in the legislature affects the time to the presence of a female executive. Cox regression models, which are used later, incorporate time-varying covariates into the baseline hazard by interacting the variable with time (Box-Steffensmeier 1996; Box-Steffensmeier and Jones 1997, 2004). It is important to note, however, that, unlike typical interaction

Table 3.3. Time to Female Executive

Variables	Model 3 All Female Executives	Std. Error	Model 4 Non-Interim Female Executives	Std. Error
Parliamentary System	1.407	0.649	2.439	1.952
South and Central America	0.142***	0.079	0.074**	0.080
North America	0.359	0.367	2.161	2.612
Africa and the Middle East	0.228***	0.120	0.362	0.309
Asia	1.155	0.439	4.639	4.167
Time Varying Covariates				
Pct. Women in the Legislature	1.001	0.001	1.001	0.001
Years since Suffrage	1.001**	0.000	1.000	0.000
Natural Log GDP per Capita	0.995	0.004	0.994	0.004
Female Labor Force Participation	1.000	0.000	1.000	0.000
Quota Law	1.010	0.008	1.023***	0.008
1980s	1.122**	0.053	1.023**	0.087
1990s	1.141**	0.060	1.212**	0.111
2000s	1.111**	0.054	1.184	0.104
Observations	3372		3372	
Wald Test	84.46***		107.76***	
Significance	0.000		0.000	

* $p < 0.10$, ** $p < 0.05$, *** $p < 0.01$

terms in political science, we do not need to include a main effect and an interactive effect to interpret the coefficient. Table 3.3 presents the results for all female executives in column two and non-interim female executives in column four. The Wald statistics at the bottom of the table serve as a joint hypothesis test that all variables are simultaneously equal to zero. We can confidently reject that hypothesis in both models.

To interpret the effect of the variables, we consider the effect on the hazard rate at a particular point in time for each time in the model. We use percentage change in the risk of a female executive to determine the effect of each variable, allowing for the percentage change to vary at different points during the study. The formula for calculating the effect of time-varying covariates is slightly different from that for the time-invariant variables (see Box-Steffensmeier 1996, Box-Steffensmeier and Jones 1997, 2004). Table 3.4 reports the percentage changes in the hazard for each of the significant variables.

Table 3.4 shows that a number of the factors included in the model increase the hazard ratio—that is, they decrease the time to the event. South and Central American countries, for example, see a female executive 15 percent faster than other regions, while the time in Africa and the Middle East is even faster—26 percent faster. For each year since women were granted the

Table 3.4. Percent Change in the Hazard Rate

Variables	All Female Executives	Non-Interim Female Executives
South and Central America	15%	8%
Africa and the Middle East	26%	N.S.
Time Varying Covariates		
Years since Suffrage (+1 year)	172%	N.S.
Quota Law	N.S.	178%
1980s	207%	221%
1990s	213%	236%
2000s	204%	N.S.

right to vote, there is a 172 percent increase in the hazard, making a female executive more likely with each year of women's political participation. Similarly, as we move forward in time, female executives become more likely with each passing decade, though the change was the greatest in the 1990s.

We see similar results for non-interim female executives. In South and Central American countries, there is an 8 percent increase in the hazard, decreasing the time to a non-interim female executive. While the effect of the decade dummy variables is not surprising, the effect of quotas is noteworthy. Once a country adopts a quota, either national or party, its likelihood of electing a non-interim female executive increases by 178 percent.

Discussion of Results

Overall, we find that a number of similar factors, including contagion, influence both the instance and the time to a female executive. The percentage of women in the legislature strongly affects the incidence and onset of a female executive. The results indicate that the election of more women to the legislature not only leads to a greater probability of a female executive but also means that a female executive will be elected sooner. Thus, contagion matters.

The effect of quotas is less clear. On the one hand, the incidence of female chief executives is positively affected by a reserved-seat or compulsory party quota, and the onset of non-interim female executives is faster where these quotas are present. On the other hand, the number of quota parties undermines the incidence of female executives. This mixed effect may tell us much about both the dynamics of quota adoption and the election of female chief executives.

The difference between parliamentary and nonparliamentary systems is also important. The broader electoral systems literature highlights the fact that female candidates perform more poorly in electoral systems that feature strong personal vote incentives. Presidential systems are defined by the fact that the chief executive is directly elected by the voters. Thus, personal vote incentives are quite strong in presidential systems. The finding that women are more likely, all else being equal, to be elected as a premier in a parliamentary system is, therefore, not surprising.

Greater traditions of women's participation are also important in determining the likelihood of women entering this office. We consistently found that countries with longer histories of suffrage were more likely to elect female executives. Yet, we found that labor force participation had the opposite effect. This, plus the finding that wealthier countries were not more or less likely to have female executives, indicates that the phenomenon of female chief executives is not more common in advanced, industrialized democracies. A simple perusal of the cases with female chief executives, both interim and non-interim, supports this conclusion.

In an effort to understand the substantive implications of these findings, we examine the known influences on a female executive in a specific country: France.

A Female President in France?

In 2007, Ségolène Royal of the Socialist Party lost in the second round of the presidential election to Nicolas Sarkozy of the Union for a People's Movement. Royal lost the election by just over 6 percent of the vote, yet she did receive the votes of more than 16 million people. As the first French female presidential candidate from a major political party, Royal and her candidacy represented a significant moment in French political history. Both Royal and Marine Le Pen of the right-wing National Front ran for the presidency in 2012 (but Royal eventually lost the Socialist Party nomination to François Hollande). Thus, for a while, it appeared possible that the 2012 French presidential campaign would feature two female candidates, one right, one left, from major French parties.

Given the possibility that France could have had two female candidates in 2012, we seek to understand whether we should expect a woman to win the French presidency. The fact that Ségolène Royal won a major party presidential nomination in 2007 could be interpreted as evidence of the rising status of women in French politics. This is especially true given that it comes on the heels of the successful passage of the Parity Bill in 2000, which created quotas for party nominations. Thus, the possibility that a woman might win the chief executive office does not seem completely out of character.

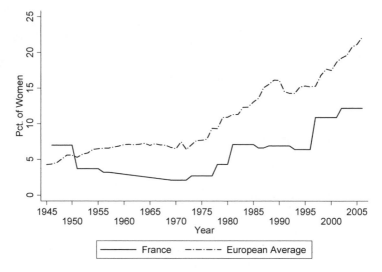

Fig. 3.4. Comparing France to Europe, 1945–2006

Yet, France maintains one of Europe's weakest records of women's legislative representation. Figure 3.4 plots the percentage of women in the French parliament and also the European average between 1945 and 2006. The data clearly demonstrate that, since 1950, the level of women's legislative representation in France is significantly lower than it is in the rest of Europe. While the 1980s began a period of increasing women's representation in France and the rest of Europe, the increases in France were much less marked than those in other European democracies. Thus, while France has made some headway by adopting a compulsory party quota and nominating a woman to run for the highest executive office, the level of women's representation suggests that these feats do not tell the complete story of the status of women in the French political system.

The existing literature suggests several reasons for the poor … record of women's legislative representation in France. Cultural factors such as the role of the Catholic Church and the historical belief that women were not able to represent the country were thought to limit women's participation (Sineau 2008). In fact, French women did not receive the right to vote and stand for office until 1944.

Another issue revolves around the universalism that formed the foundation of republican France. Allwood and Wadi (2004) argue that republican France embraced gender-neutral constructs of citizens. Thus, the recognition of political divisions by gender would represent a step away from the preferred universalism of gender-neutral policies. It was only in the early

1990s that feminists began to argue that this approach prevented the recognition of important gender imbalances that only created more obstacles to finding solutions for them (Allwood and Wadi 2004).

Others point to the weak mobilization of the women's movement to address the gender imbalance in the French parliament. Until the 1990s, women's groups were active politically; however, they did not mobilize to erase this gender imbalance (Mazur 2001). Women's groups simply paid more attention to other issues on their agendas. Efforts to increase women's legislative representation came primarily from the political parties, in particular the Socialist Party (Krook 2005). Thus, a focus on women's representation did not begin to develop more broadly until the 1990s.

The electoral system may also pose an obstacle for women's representation. France uses a single-member district majoritarian system to elect the National Assembly. If no candidate receives at least 50 percent of the vote, a second-round runoff election occurs, featuring those candidates with at least 12.5 percent of the vote (or the top two vote-getters if no two receive at least 12.5 percent). This system creates the type of personal vote incentives that undermine women's representation (Sineau 2008; Thiébault 1988). French parties also remain reluctant to both nominate women and adopt measures to deal with women's underrepresentation (Appleton and Mazur 1993; Sineau 2008).

The difficulties faced by women in French electoral politics demonstrate for some actors the logic behind the Parity Law adopted in June 2000. The weak record of women's membership in the National Assembly surely pushed women's activists to demand a compulsory quota to help change the situation of women in parliament. However, it is not clear to all researchers that a demand for gender parity influenced French legislators to adopt such a law. Frechette, Maniquet, and Morelli (2008) argue that the adoption of the quota actually increased the male incumbency advantage in French elections. Thus, the Parity Law offered an opportunity to further entrench male incumbents by boosting their reelection chances. The fact that the law failed to improve women's representation significantly after its introduction supports this contention.

An understanding of women's underrepresentation in the French National Assembly has, according to our empirical analysis of female chief executives, important implications for determining whether France is likely to elect a female chief executive. Two features stand out from our statistical analysis and from Table 3.5 about the French case that undermine the likelihood of a female executive—the number of years since suffrage and the percentage of women in the legislature. Both of these variables are strongly correlated with the likelihood of a female chief executive. Yet, France fairs poorly on both counts in comparison with other European democracies. France extended universal suffrage in 1944, more than twelve years later than the average European country in our sample (1932.9).

In addition, our statistical analyses found that the percentage of women in the legislature was strongly correlated with the probability of a female executive. Thus, contagion clearly matters in the election of female executives. To make clearer the implications of our contagion argument, we simulate the impact of different levels of women's representation on the probability of a non-interim female chief executive in France. To do this, we estimate the predicted probability of a female executive using the results from Model 2 in Table 3.1, setting all variables at their actual French values in the year, which includes the presence of a national quota law. We then estimate the predicted probability of a female executive where we set the percentage women in the legislature variable at its European average, while setting all other variables at their French levels. We also plot the 90 percent confidence interval around our estimates.

Figure 3.5 presents the results of our simulation. The observed predicted probability is low, never reaching more than 0.5 percent. Thus, the baseline probability of a non-interim French female executive is small. The results show that increasing the percentage women in the legislature to the European average does raise the probability of a non-interim female executive in France for each year, beginning in 1965. However, the difference between the simulated probabilities and the observed probabilities is not great. In fact, the 90 percent confidence intervals overlap, suggesting that it is difficult to conclude definitively that raising the percentage of women in the legislature to the European average would make a difference in the probability of electing a female executive.

To push the analysis further, we plot the simulated predicted probability of a female non-interim chief executive in France over the range of percentage of women in the legislature (0 to 100). We set all other values at their observed French levels. Figure 3.6 presents these predictions with the 90 percent confidence interval for all estimates. The simulated predicted

Table 3.5. Comparing France to Europe, 1945–2006

Variable	France Avg.	European Avg.	Difference	P Value
Log of District Magnitude	9.648	8.966	0.682	0.000
Female Labor Force Participation	54.142	58.135	3.993	0.003
Years Since Suffrage	31.500	44.146	12.646	0.000
Percent Women in the Legislature	5.557	11.981	6.424	0.000

Note: P values from a difference of means t-test.

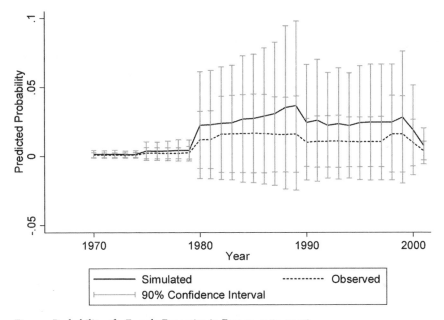

Fig. 3.5. Probability of a Female Executive in France, 1965–2006

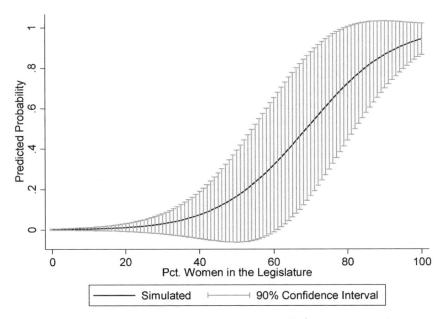

Fig. 3.6. Probability of a Female Executive in France as Women's Representation Increases

probabilities increase as the level of women's representation increases. Given our contagion argument and the statistical analysis we presented earlier, this relationship is to be expected. We need to recognize, however, that the estimates do not become statistically significant until the percentage of women in the legislature reaches 61 percent. We have no countries in our sample, including France with its Parity Law, that reach this level.

Conclusion

While some of the factors known to affect women's representation as national executive found here are familiar to those who work in this area of study, other findings are more ground-breaking. The years since suffrage, the country's level of development, and time all influence the likelihood that a country will have a female executive, though results vary by the non-interim and all executive models. It is not surprising that as we move forward in time, the probability of a female executive goes up, even without any other changes in a country's circumstances. Greater awareness of women's political representation, or lack thereof, certainly plays a role in greater participation by women, not only through recruitment but also through acceptance of female candidates. The finding holds true for both the models predicting the presence of a female executive and the models measuring time to a female executive.

Similarly, as women increasingly participate in public life, as measured through the vote, the probability of a female executive increases over time. This means that countries with a greater tradition of women's participation are more likely to see a female executive.

Development's effect on women's representation, however, cuts a different way. Surprisingly, the most developed countries and the countries where more women participate in the labor force are less likely to have a female executive. While the finding runs counter to expectation, it is consistent with what we know about female executives in the developed world—they are rare. Perhaps, as Matland (1998) argued, our understanding of the effect of development on women's representation should be reconsidered.

We also find strong evidence that contagion influences the election of female chief executives. The influence of women's participation in the legislature on women executives is perhaps the most significant finding from this analysis. While we are hardly the first to consider the possibility of an effect for other institutions, our models account for the year-to-year effect of women's representation in one institution on other institutions. Past models (see Jalalzai 2008) considered the effect of legislative representation on the likelihood of a female executive *at any point in the study*. This, however, does not accurately portray the influence of contagion. For one institution to influence another, the event must be relatively recent. The importance of women building a substantial presence in one political institution and having that presence spill over into another institution is the creation of a tradition of women's participation in the country, supplying a pool of candidates to serve in various offices. In order to understand the effect, a comprehensive measure of the influence of legislative participation on executive participation is necessary.

Not only do we find that legislative participation influences the likelihood of executive participation; we also find that the presence of a quota law can influence both the incidence of a female executive and the time to a female executive. Female executives are more likely and their time to power is shorter in countries that adopt quota laws. This suggests that the path to a female president or prime minister may be through other political institutions and that those interested in seeing female executives must start by recruiting women to hold legislative seats or working to adopt quotas, at the party or the national level. This result, moreover, is further proof of the contagion of women's representation.

4

Gender and Cross-National Courts

With the confirmation of Elena Kagan as Associate Justice, in 2010, the U.S. Supreme Court for the first time in history included three women. Given that only four women have ever served on the Court in its long history, the dramatic increase from 11 percent female to 33 percent female under the Obama administration is noteworthy. President George W. Bush had several opportunities to appoint women and indeed also had the support of his wife and retiring Justice Sandra Day O'Connor to do so, yet he failed to appoint any women to the high court. Perhaps the election of President Barack Obama marks a change in women's political representation on the bench.

Around the globe, women's representation on high courts has risen in recent decades, but the total number of women on the courts is still highly variable. In 2006–2007, among OECD countries, the percentage of seats on high courts held by women varied from 0 percent to 60 percent (Williams and Thames 2008). Thus, as in our previous chapters, we find evidence of significant variation in gender equity for democratic institutions cross-nationally.

Given the importance of high courts to democracy itself, this range raises the question of what explains the variation.

In this chapter, we show that, in part, variation in the level of women's representation in other democratic institutions explains the variation in women's high court representation. In this case, we find evidence that women's legislative representation is correlated with the number of seats held by women on high courts. Our results, however, are limited to more developed countries. This suggests that the impact of contagion is less robust when explaining women's court representation.

This chapter proceeds as follows. First, we review the existing literature on women's representation on courts. Here we demonstrate how the logic that explains the election of women to legislatures or as a chief executive differs from the logic that explains women's participation on courts. Second, we explain why we believe that contagion will affect women's representation on courts. In particular, we examine the role of women's legislative representation. Third, we undertake a statistical analysis of female court representation. We extend this analysis by a detailed discussion of women's representation on courts in Japan, which demonstrates the importance of contagion as a predictor of women's accession to seats on courts. Finally, we conclude with a discussion of the relevance of our analysis to our contagion argument with regard to courts.

Factors Affecting Representation on the Bench

The factors that influence women's representation on high courts are largely drawn from those that influence women's representation in other political institutions. Social, economic, and political factors all influence women's representation on the bench. Perhaps most significant, however, is the potential for contagion to influence women's service on the bench. Judiciaries, unlike many other political offices, are often chosen by the members of the other two branches of government. This increased opportunity to influence the composition of an institution of government makes the representation of women in executive and legislative positions all the more important. How these factors align to influence women's representation on the courts is our next consideration.

Other studies examining women's representation, including those that specifically look at the courts, find that two main types of factors influence women's representation: the characteristics of the person (called supply-side factors) and the characteristics of the institution or country (called demand-side factors) (Williams and Thames 2008). While women's experiences in the legal profession undoubtedly influence their willingness to seek a seat on the bench (for an example from the United States, see Williams 2008, 2009), these factors are outside the bounds of this work. Women's professional backgrounds, their ambition for the bench, and their recruitment are all important factors worthy of study. These micro-level explanations, however, do not lend themselves well to cross-national analysis. This is not to say that supply-side factors are unrelated to demand-side influences. Past work has shown that seeing other women participate in political life generates ambition among those not yet participating in public life (Escobar-Lemmon and Taylor-Robinson 2005).

The demand-side influences on women's representation on the courts include the factors most familiar to those working on representation more generally. Women's participation in the workforce, their participation in political life within the country, a country's wealth, the selection mechanism for choosing judges, and the types of courts all influence women's representation on the bench. Countries that are wealthier, with a greater tradition of women's participation, are more likely to see women serving on the court (Williams and Thames 2008).

Why the Bench Is Different

The importance of selection mechanisms and the variation in court types demonstrate that our understanding of representation is incomplete if we focus exclusively on the popularly elected branches of government. To begin, the selection of judges for high courts is entirely an elite process; the only variation is in who appoints judges or can influence appointments. Past studies of the judiciary have shown that appointive systems, especially when the selector is particularly sympathetic to women's representation, can substantially increase the number of women on the bench (Slotnick 1984; Williams and Thames 2008). In the United States, for example, a sympathetic president or a powerful senator can serve the interests of women's representation. Selection in other countries, however, is a far more diverse process. Typically, formal power for selecting judges rests with the executive or legislative branch. However, institutions that can influence women's representation (e.g., by generating the list from which an executive must choose) range from the monarchy to the Ministry of Justice to specially selected committees (much like merit selection committees), all of which can influence the executive or legislative selectors. While the entirety of the process is not easily captured, a consideration of these additional influences is important to understanding women's representation on courts.

Not only are other countries diverse in their process for choosing judges for high courts, but they also vary in the extent to which they divide power among several high courts. The U.S. Supreme Court handles both constitutional and procedural issues that arise in the federal courts. Other countries, however, have separate courts for handling appeals from the lower courts, constitutional issues, and administrative issues. While division of the responsibilities of the judiciary creates more seats (and thus more opportunities) for women, the representation of women across these institutions may not be even. Women may be better represented on less prestigious administrative courts than on the most prestigious constitutional courts, which may be without women (Anasagasti and Wuiame 1999; Kenney 1998/1999, 2002; Linehan 2001; Williams and Thames 2008). The variation in power and prestige of courts outside the United States (as documented in the works of Epstein, Knight, and Shvetsova 2001; Herron and Randazzo 2003; Schwartz 1998; Smithey and Ishiyama 2000, 2002) may influence women's representation on the bench. Of course, the presence of a transnational judiciary marks the ultimate step in a judicial career ladder for many countries, with judges serving on courts within a country as a stepping stone to the transnational court (Kenney 2002).

Why Contagion Is Important

Both variations in the type of court and variations in selection mechanisms create the potential for contagion to be a factor influencing women's representation on high courts. Judges are chosen by groups that have become increasingly diverse over time. In part, this diversity is driven by the use of quotas and by a greater awareness of the importance of women's representation in political life. It is therefore not only possible but likely that increased diversity in other political institutions and the presence of quota laws will increase women's representation on the bench, as well. The effect of a more diverse selecting body is obvious; as women's numbers in other institutions increase, a critical mass of those interested in women's representation will form, increasing the possibility that gender will be a criterion in filling seats on the bench. The effect of quotas, however, is more indirect. Quota laws serve to increase the number of women in parties and legislatures, not on the bench per se. However, past work has shown that quotas have an unintended effect, increasing women's representation on the bench (Williams and Thames 2008). There is some facial validity to the effect; quotas increase the diversity of the selectors and raise awareness of women's political participation, which can increase the number of women serving in other institutions, as well. While the findings of previous work applied only to advanced, industrialized countries in a more limited sample, the expectation holds for a more diverse group of countries, as well.

Why Representation Matters for Courts

Whether or not contagion matters, and we think that it does, understanding the factors that influence women's representation is important regardless of what those factors are. Courts are inherently antidemocratic institutions. Without ties to the people, courts risk the possibility that the very legitimacy of what they do can be suspect to those who do not understand the judicial process. This suspicion of the judiciary, as of any political institution, becomes more pronounced when groups are excluded from participation, and this is especially true for women (Pitkin 1972). Not only is there no electoral connection to tie the disenfranchised to the political body (Phillips 1995), but judges are far more difficult to remove from office than are other appointed officials. Cabinets can be dissolved and ministers dismissed, but judges can serve for life or, at the very least a long term; removal is a complicated process typically prompted by a major ethical violation, not by public dissatisfaction with their rulings. In fact, one could go so far as to say that removing judges one dislikes because of their decision making is an infringement on judicial independence.

Because of the difficulty of removing judges from office, the choice of who serves on a court becomes all the more important. The decisions of judges are binding, and past work has shown that the individual characteristics of judges, as well as their institutional context, can influence their decision making. Individual attitudes and personal characteristics all influence the decision making of judges (for examples outside the United States, see Schubert 1977; for examples within the United States, see Segal and Spaeth 2002; Tate 1981; Tate and Handberg 1991). Gender is among the factors that may influence decision making, with some studies finding that female judges decide cases differently from their male counterparts, especially when women's-rights issues are before the court (Allen and Wall 1987; Boyd, Epstein, and Martin 2010; Gruhl, Spohn, and Welch 1981; Gryski, Main, and Dixon 1986; Songer and Crews-Meyer 2000; Songer, Davis, and Haire 1994; Walker and Barrow 1985). The evidence, however, is mixed (see, e.g., Davis 1992; Sisk, Heise, and Morriss 1998; Westergren 2004). Those interested in studying women's representation outside the United States also expect gender to influence decision making, thus explaining women's representation on courts dealing with human rights issues (Linehan 2001).

Participation on High Courts

Examining the behavior of high court judges across the globe is an interesting line of inquiry, but one that must be put aside for the time being. If we do
not first understand the factors that affect the representation of women on
the bench, our understanding of decision making is at best incomplete. We
must first consider the characteristics of the courts and of the countries in
which they sit to understand the environment in which these women come
to make decisions. To understand that question, we examined women's representation on high courts in countries around the world. High courts here
are defined as constitutional, administrative, and appellate courts of last re-
sort within the country. Because of the division of judicial functions around
the world, this means we must look at multiple courts for some countries. To
find the number of women serving on a particular court, as well the methods
of selection, number of seats, and term limits, we examined the Web pages
of the court. If the information was not available or if it was unclear, we con-
tacted the administrative office for the court or the Ministry of Justice.

While we could have continued to examine the representation of women
on courts in advanced countries, we decided to expand the analysis for this
chapter. There are two reasons for this expansion. First, in the years since our
previous study, the number of women on high courts in advanced countries
may not have changed much, the U.S. case aside. Vacancies on these courts
are quite rare, meaning that the opportunity to increase women's representation may not have come up. Second, looking only at advanced countries
truncates the effect of some of the independent variables of interest, including a country's wealth and its tradition of women's political participation.
By going outside the OECD, we allow for greater variation in all the factors
known to influence women's participation.

This is not to say that we have complete information on women's representation on high courts. For a number of countries, we were missing information about the number of women or the method of selection for choosing judges. Without the information, we had to drop the country from the
analysis. Thus, while the information presented is more comprehensive than
anything else published thus far, it is far from complete.

Table 4.1 shows the current state of women's representation on each type
of court. The information in Table 4.1 demonstrates several points that merit
highlighting. First, there is a significant amount of variation in women's participation in high courts that is worth explaining. This is true across court
types, as well as within a country or region. The percentage of women serving on high courts ranges from a low of zero percent on several courts to

Table 4.1. Women's Participation by Court

Country	Constitutional Court	Single High Court	High Court of Appeals	Administrative Court
Albania	22%	—	50%	—
Angola	43%	—	—	—
Argentina	—	29%	—	—
Australia	—	43%	—	—
Austria	29%	—	—	16%
Bangladesh	—	0%	—	—
Belgium	0%	—	—	—
Belize	—	0%	—	—
Benin	29%	—	—	—
Bolivia	20%	—	17%	—
Bosnia & Herzegovina	22%	—	—	—
Canada	—	44%	—	—
Cape Verde	—	40%	—	—
Chile	10%	—	—	—
Colombia	9%	—	13%	—
Costa Rica	—	14%	—	—
Croatia	38%	—	—	—
Cyprus	—	8%	—	—
Czech Republic	33%	—	—	—
Dominican Republic	—	31%	—	—
Ecuador	22%	—	—	—
Estonia	—	16%	—	—
Finland	—	26%	—	—
France	18%	—	29%	—
Georgia	33%	—	—	—
Germany	19%	—	22%	—
Honduras	—	20%	—	—
Hungary	0%	—	—	—
Iceland	—	11%	—	—
India	—	3%	—	—
Indonesia	11%	—	—	—
Ireland	—	25%	—	—
Israel	—	21%	—	—
Italy	—	7%	—	—
Japan	—	13%	—	—
Latvia	43%	—	—	—
Lithuania	22%	—	—	—
Luxembourg	—	51%	—	—
Madagascar	33%	—	—	—
Mexico	—	18%	—	—
Morocco	0%	—	—	—
Netherlands	—	42%	—	—
New Zealand	—	20%	—	—
Norway	—	35%	—	—
Peru	0%	—	—	—
Philippines	—	27%	—	—
Poland	27%	—	8%	—
Portugal	31%	—	—	—
Republic of Korea	0%	—	17%	—
Russian Federation	5%	—	—	—
Singapore	—	—	—	—
Slovakia	20%	—	18%	—
Slovenia	44%	—	—	—
South Africa	27%	—	—	—
Spain	17%	—	—	—
Sweden	—	38%	—	—
Switzerland	—	26%	—	—
Turkey	13%	—	—	—
Ukraine	10%	—	—	—
United Kingdom	—	8%	—	—
United States	—	33%	—	—
Venezuela	—	41%	—	—
Zimbabwe	—	0%	—	—
Average	20%	23%	22%	16%

a high of 51 percent on the Supreme Court of Luxembourg, with an average women's representation of 22 percent across all courts. Second, there are a number of courts, disproportionately administrative courts, on which no information could be found.[1] Despite the overall rarity of administrative courts in the countries in our sample, the missing information might affect the results of the analysis. Administrative courts tend to be filled by civil servants and are a type of court that may be more likely to include women (Williams and Thames 2008). Thus, it is important to remember in the analysis that follows that the results may understate women's participation because they do not include full information on administrative courts. This not to say, however, that the results are not representative of women's participation on other court types.

To understand the factors affecting the variation on these courts, we collected information on the country and court. Country-specific factors include those used throughout this book: the natural log of GDP per capita in constant U.S. dollars, women's labor force participation, years since women were granted suffrage, and the contagion factors of the percentage of women in the legislature and the presence of a quota law of any type.[2] Many of these factors measure the openness of a country to women's participation in public life. Our two measures for contagion, women's participation in the legislature and the presence of a quota law, are already factors known to influence women's participation in other avenues of public life (Escobar-Lemmon and Taylor-Robinson 2005; Williams and Thames 2008). Not only do women in the legislature often choose or at least influence the selection of judges; they also make women's participation in public life more salient to those who choose judges. Similarly, quotas raise awareness of women's representation, regardless of the type of quota within the country.[3] The presence of more women in the legislature and of a quota both likely increase the presence of women on high courts. The years since women were granted the right to vote is indicative of the tradition of women's political participation in the country. We expect that the longer the length of time since suffrage, the more women will be serving on courts.

In addition to the measures of contagion, we included variables accounting for the GDP per capita in the country, as well as the participation of women in the labor force. We expect that the higher the GDP in the country and the greater women's representation in the labor force, the more likely women are to participate on high courts. Women will have developed the tools for participating in public life by working outside the home and will have more opportunities for education and career in countries that have a higher GDP.

We collected information on the presence of life terms or mandatory retirement for the judges on the courts we studied, as well as the number of seats on the court and the method of selection for judges for that court. Life terms, mandatory retirement, and the number of seats are all thought to be indicators of the prestige of the court (Epstein, Knight, and Shvetsova 2001; Herron and Randazzo 2003). Judges who serve with the protections of life tenure are thought to be more independent from the other institutions of government and have more institutional power. Mandatory retirement is also thought to protect the quality of judges serving on the bench. Seats on the bench not only are an indicator of prestige but also speak to the opportunities women have for serving on the bench. Dichotomous variables are used for life term and mandatory retirement, while a continuous measure is included for the number of seats on the bench.

Method of selection is a more complicated measure to include. The selection of judges for high courts often involves a more complex process than the final selection by the executive, the most well-known stage in the selection process. The variation in institutions involved in the selection of judges may influence women's representation. First, selectors, especially unitary actors like executives, may seek electoral advantage for their attempts to diversify the bench (Slotnick 1984). There is a lot of variation in the selection of judges for the high courts of the countries shown in Table 4.1, with legislatures, ministries of justice, special selection committees, and other judges all potentially involved in the selection process (see Wood 2007 for a more complete explanation). Moreover, there are a significant number of additional stages to the selection process, with some countries using a committee or the legislature to make a list of candidates from which an executive must choose a nominee. Other countries have the more traditional selection mechanism of executive choice with legislative approval. A final variation on selection breaks up the seats on the bench to provide an opportunity for a number of different actors to choose some portion of the judges for the bench (e.g., three seats chosen by the executive, three by the legislature, and three by other judges). Because selection by the executive was reasonably common, we used a dichotomous measure of executive selection.[4] All other selection types are the excluded category.

To estimate the effects of these independent variables on the number of women serving on high courts, we estimated negative binomial models. These models are appropriate for count data in the presence of overdispersion, often found with groups (Williams and Thames 2008). Included in the models are measures of the number of seats on each court, preventing the representation of women on larger courts from unduly influencing the results. Separate models were estimated on the basis of the countries included in our 2008 study to compare the differences in results due to an expanded sample. It should be noted, however, that the countries new to this analysis are an unusual grouping of those on which data are available. The convenience of the sample may limit the generalizability of the results. Table 4.2 shows the results of the analyses.

The models show the effects for the factors we have discussed as influencing women's representation on high courts. For each sample of the data, two sets of models were estimated. The first set examines representation on all courts together, while the second includes variables that control for the type of court on which women were serving, with single high court as the baseline for the model. The numbers of countries at the bottom of the table are really groups into which the data are organized. In reality, there are 229 women holding seats out of a possible 1,011 positions on these courts.

The first conclusion we reach from the model is that the two samples lead to slightly different results for some of the factors. While the number of seats on the bench is significant across all models, the percentage of women in the legislature, the percentage of women in the labor force, and the years since women were given the right to vote vary in their significance. Each of these three measures had significantly higher means in the original sample than in the expanded sample, not surprising given the differences in development

Table 4.2. Factors Affecting Women's Representation on High Courts

| Variables | Original Countries | | | | Expanded Sample | | | |
| | Model 1 | | Model 2 | | Model 3 | | Model 4 | |
	Coeff.	Std. Err.	Coeff.	Std. Err.	Coeff.	Std. Err.	Coeff.	Std. Err.
Seats	0.054***	0.012	0.051***	0.014	0.068***	0.009	0.067***	0.011
Pct. Women	0.024*	0.012	0.026*	0.015	0.008	0.008	0.008	0.008
Quota Law	−0.593	0.379	−0.579	0.467	0.009	0.203	0.003	0.204
Labor Force Part.	−0.005	0.015	−0.008	0.017	0.021**	0.009	0.021**	0.009
GDP per Capita	−0.000	0.000	−0.000	0.000	0.000	0.000	0.000	0.000
Years since Suffrage	−0.004	0.007	0.004	0.007	0.009**	0.004	0.010**	0.004
Life Terms	0.439***	0.209	0.328	0.297	−0.071	0.186	−0.140	0.214
Mandatory Ret.	−0.526**	0.25	−0.555**	0.269	−0.401**	0.179	−0.371**	0.183
Presidential App.	0.185	0.195	0.211	0.211	0.286*	0.167	0.217	0.180
Court of Appeals			−0.043	0.346			0.323	0.295
Constitutional Court			−0.169	0.149			−0.090	0.212
Constant	0.483	1.336	0.757	1.492	−1.926**	0.589	−1.962**	0.677
LN Alpha	−16.564	0.651	−16.518	−1.427	−15.603	2.953	−15.893	1.895
Alpha	0.000	0.000	0.000	0.000	0.000	0.000	0.000	0.000
Countries	29		29		47		47	

*** $p < 0.01$; ** $p < 0.05$; * $p < 0.10$

between the two groups. While a number of the differences have been accounted for in the model, group differences may continue to drive the results. Future studies should consider this. Finally, the countries included in the expanded sample are not necessarily those with strong traditions of judicial independence. In Argentina, a country included in the expanded sample, the Supreme Court has struggled to escape the influence of the executive. While some of the traditional measures of judicial independence are included, not all can be, and their absence may influence the results. Future analyses should consider expanding on both the sample and the model used here.

Despite the differences across models, there are additional conclusions to discuss. Clearly, the total number of seats is an important predictor of women's success on high courts. Where women have more opportunity to serve on these courts, more women are serving. Additionally, mandatory retirement tends to hinder women's representation on high courts, likely because women tend to enter public life at a later date and may not be considered viable candidates because of their age. The percentage of women in the legislature and the percentage of women in the labor force, while significant in different models, are both in the expected direction. Higher percentages of women serving in these areas of public life increase women's participation on the bench. This means that both traditions of women's participation and our understanding of contagion are influencing women serving on the bench. Finally, both life terms and presidential appointment increase women's representation on the high courts in some countries. To better understand the

Table 4.3. Predicted Probabilities

Variable	Original Countries		Expanded Sample	
	Model 1	Model 2	Model 3	Model 4
Seats (+1 std. dev.)	3.4	4.0	2.9	3.1
Seats (−1 std. dev.)	2.6	3.1	2.1	2.3
Percent Women in Legislature (+1 std. dev.)	4.0	4.8	N.S.	N.S.
Percent Women in Legislature (−1 std. dev.)	2.7	3.1	N.S.	N.S.
Percent Women in Labor Force (+1 std. dev.)	N.S.	N.S.	3.1	3.3
Percent Women in Labor Force (−1 std. dev.)	N.S.	N.S.	2.5	2.7
Years since Female Suffrage (+1 std. dev.)	N.S.	N.S.	3.3	3.6
Years since Female Suffrage (−1 std. dev.)	N.S.	N.S.	2.6	2.7
Life Terms	5.1	N.S.	N.S.	N.S.
Mandatory Retirement	1.9	2.1	1.9	2.0
Presidential Appointment	N.S.	N.S.	3.7	N.S.
Baseline	3.2	3.7	2.8	3.0

impact of these variables, predicted probabilities were estimated (Tomz, Wittenberg, and King 2003).

It is worth noting at the outset that none of the predictions for these models includes a substantial number of women. However, with an average court of fourteen people, having three to five women serving means that 21 percent to 36 percent of the bench is composed of women, hardly an insubstantial amount. The differences across predictions are not huge, but they can substantially change the proportion of women serving on the bench. The difference between one standard deviation below the mean and one standard deviation above the mean for seats on the court is the difference of about one women serving on the court. The same is true for the difference in the percentage of women in the legislature, though the difference is slightly greater than one. Life terms appear to substantially increase the number of women on the bench, with 1.5 times more women serving in countries with life terms. Those countries with mandatory retirement have one fewer woman serving on the bench, all else being equal.

While the differences across predictions are interesting, it is necessary to go a step further to determine the impact of these factors on women's representation on high courts and predict when women will reach parity.

Women Judges and the Supreme Court of Japan

The Japanese Supreme Court did not contain a woman until 1994, when Takashi Hisako was appointed to the bench. While several women have served since Hisako's appointment, the number of women on Japan's highest court remains small. The dearth of women found on the court is also the case in many other areas of Japanese political and economic life (Usui, Rose, and Kageyma 2003).

The House of Representatives, the lower house of the National Diet of Japan, is no exception. Women did not obtain the right of suffrage or the ability to stand for election until 1946. In the first Japanese election in which women participated, fifteen women won seats, making up 3.2 percent of the new Diet. Women would not compose more than 3.2 percent of the House until fifty years later, in 1996, when women won 4.6 percent of the seats. Figure 4.1 plots the percentage of women in the Japanese House of Representatives from 1956 to 2006 and compares it to the figures for the world and to the European averages for the same period. The results clearly indicate that Japan has, over this period, lagged behind not only Europe but the rest of the world in terms of women's legislative representation.

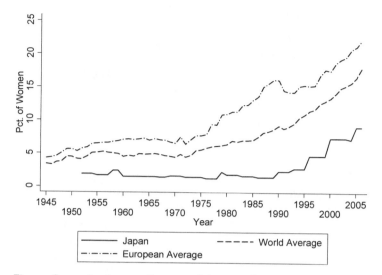

Fig. 4.1. Comparing Japan to Europe and the Rest of the World

What explains the weak Japanese record on women's representation? For some observers, cultural and historical factors create deeply held gendered stereotypes that limit women's roles to the home, keeping them out of politics (Darcy and Nixon 1996; Sheel 2003; Usui, Rose, and Kageyma 2003). The weight of culture, therefore, undermines the election of women to the legislature. The gendered occupational roles translate into fewer women able to find positions in high-status occupations, which often translate into electoral success (Christensen 2008). Thus, the pool of quality female candidates is potentially much smaller than the pool of men.

For some researchers, the electoral system is also to blame. Until 1993, Japan employed a single nontransferable vote system. In this system, candidates competed for office in multimember districts where votes accrued to individual candidates and not to parties. Thus, parties often nominated multiple candidates, creating a strong basis for intra-party competition. This system creates strong personal vote incentives, making much of a candidate's electoral success dependent upon his or her own resources and qualities. Parties often had limited impact or control over their candidates (Christensen 2008). Thus, successful candidates often relied upon personal connections to raise sufficient funds to win (Christensen 2008; Iwanaga 2003; Sheel 2003). Not surprisingly, this system created strong incumbency advantages that reduced legislative turnover, both factors that have been found to undermine women's legislative representation in other countries (Usui, Rose, and Kageyma 2003).[5]

Japan instituted significant electoral reform after 1993. The adoption of a mixed-member majoritarian system that paired a closed-list proportional-representation election with single-member district elections offered new opportunities for women. While women remain disadvantaged in the single-member district elections, they have found more success in the proportional-representation elections. In fact, the adoption of a proportional-representation tier is credited with increasing the number of female Diet members (Christensen 2008; Iwanaga 2003).

Some researchers argue that Japan's poor record of women's representation can be blamed on the unwillingness of parties, particularly the dominant Liberal Democratic Party of Japan (LDP), to nominate women. Iwanaga (2003) argues that the LDP consistently nominated women in marginal constituencies, limiting their opportunities to win. Christensen (2008) argues that the LDP was not against nominating women; however, the Japanese electoral system makes it difficult for the party to push female candidacies.

Table 4.4 compares the averages of Japanese cases with the averages for the rest of our sample cases. On the one hand, Japan is wealthier and has a higher percentage of female labor force participation, on average, than the rest of our sample. On the other hand, the Japanese observations in our sample are both below average in terms of years since suffrage and the percentage of women's legislative participation. On the surface, these figures present a mixed picture concerning the representation of women among high court judges.

We argue that contagion is a critical factor that explains the number of female high court judges. Japan offers a very interesting case by which to examine the impact of contagion, because it is above average in terms of wealth and labor force participation but well below average in terms of women's legislative representation. To extend our analysis, we simulate the number of female high court judges in Japan over the range of possible percentages of

Table 4.4. Japan in Comparison to the World

Variable	Japan	World	Difference	P-value
Years since Suffrage	34	42.2	8.20	0.004
Labor Force Participation	56.8	53.6	3.2	0.034
Log GDP per Capita	10.1	8.2	1.9	0.000
Pct. Women in the Legislature	2.7	9.5	6.8	0.000

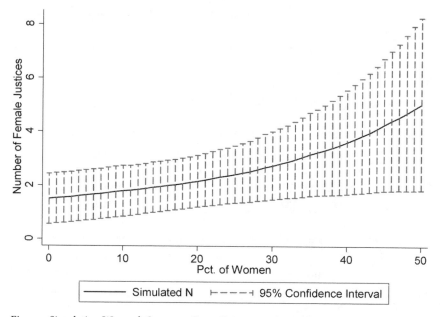

Fig. 4.2. Simulating Women's Supreme Court Representation in Japan

women in the legislature (Tomz, Wittenberg, and King 2003). We set the remaining variables at their averages for our Japanese observations. The simulation is based on the results of Model 1 in Table 4.2.

Figure 4.2 plots the simulated number of female high court judges we would expect in Japan over values of the percentage of women in the legislature. We also plot the 95 percent confidence interval around our simulated results. The results of our simulation are quite striking—as the level of women in the legislature increases, we would expect an increased number of women serving on the high court. The prediction is statistically significant for all values. Even with no women in the legislature, our model would predict at least one female high court judge. Our results show that women's legislative representation could have a strong impact on the level of women's high court representation in Japan. Thus, increasing the number of women in the Japanese Diet would have a positive impact on the number of women on the Japanese Supreme Court.

Women's representation in the legislature significantly influences women's participation on the bench in developed countries. The influence of legislatures in the selection of judges is likely the cause of this phenomenon. As legislatures become more diverse, we should see more women on high courts. Japan is a key example of this. Despite its status as a highly developed country with a significant number of women participating in the labor force, Japan lags behind Europe and the rest of the world in women's participation in political institutions. In part, this lack of participation may reflect other aspects of Japanese life.

The lack of a tradition of women's participation in Japan is affecting women's representation both in the legislature and on the Supreme Court. Other factors associated with the Japanese Supreme Court may be playing a role, as well. Judges on the Supreme Court in Japan do not have life tenure and face mandatory retirement, two factors related to women's participation. While life term would increase women's participation, mandatory retirement hinders it, creating a second strike against women serving on the Japanese Supreme Court. Moreover, Japanese judges are chosen by the monarch in consultation with the cabinet. Another method of appointment would be more likely to increase women's participation.

Nonetheless, there is hope for Japanese women who want to be Supreme Court judges. The high number of seats on the bench (fifteen) should lead to higher levels of participation by women. If the number of women in the Diet increases significantly in the next few years, we are likely to see more women on the Supreme Court.

Conclusion

The presence of women on high courts and in other democratic institutions has increased over time in many countries. Yet, we still see significant variation in women's representation on high courts cross-nationally. In this chapter, we sought to apply our contagion argument to women's high court representation. We found evidence that variation among countries on this variable was explained, in part, by variation in women's legislative representation. As the number of women in the legislature increased, so did the number of women holding seats on high courts. Thus, the contagion process that we found to be affecting women's legislative and executive representation also affects women's judicial representation. Our findings, however, are limited because we found little evidence of contagion outside the OECD.

While contagion matters, we did find several interesting additional factors that explain the variation in women's high court representation. Women are more likely to serve on courts with a greater number of seats. In addition, we found that mandatory retirement undermines women's judicial representation. We also found limited evidence that women's labor force participation, our proxy for women's political activity, increased women's judicial representation, as well.

5

Contagion and the Adoption of Voluntary Party Quotas

At a November 2008 meeting of the National Women's Council in Dublin, Ireland, Margot Wallström, vice president of the European Commission, expressed her support for gender quotas, stating that "Quotas are not an offence to women as we have enough qualified people among us; they re-balance an imbalance that comes with men choosing men" (Newenham 2008, p. 5). Wallström's comment highlights one major obstacle to increasing women's representation—the tendency of parties to nominate men at the expense of women. As discussed in previous chapters, this tendency is often reinforced by other systemic or institutional factors, such as the electoral system. Nonetheless, the continuing legislative gender gap does raise the question of how we overcome the obstacle to women's representation posed by political parties.

One potential solution is for parties to adopt voluntary gender quotas that require them to reserve a portion of their slate of candidates for women.[1] Such quotas, by increasing the number of women candidates, should increase the number of women elected. Previous research has shown this to be true (Caul 2001; Kittilson 2006). Parties that mandate a certain percentage of female candidates are more likely to elect women, increasing the overall percentage of women in the legislature.

If these quotas do in fact increase women's representation, then it begs this question: why do some parties adopt gender quotas, whereas others do not? This is a particularly important question, given the often intense debate over quotas. For some, voluntary gender quotas grant ballot access to women who would not otherwise be able to achieve it. For others, quotas discriminate against one group, in this case men, by giving another group privileged access. While debates over quotas may be ardent, the number of political parties adopting voluntary quotas has increased over time. Between 1970 and 2006, the number of parties in democratic countries with a voluntary quota increased from none to ninety-three. Thus, the question has become increasingly important. The existing research argues that the percentage of women in the party leadership, the adoption of quotas by other parties in the system, and the ideological position of parties are all critical factors that impact quota adoption (Caul 2001; Kittilson 2006).

We seek to extend this work by examining how contagion affects both the onset and the incidence of voluntary party quotas. We want to determine whether the magnitude of women's representation in other democratic institutions impacts party decisions to adopt quotas. We find that, while the presence of a female executive has little impact on the existence of voluntary party quotas, the level of women's legislative representation does have an effect on the likelihood that a party will impose quotas. We also show the critical role played by the number of parties in a country that adopt quotas. As the number of parties with quotas in a society increases, so does the likelihood that other parties will also adopt quotas. Thus, we find more evidence of contagion—as other institutions increase their commitment to gender equity, the probability that a political party will adopt a quota increases, as well.

We begin this chapter by defining voluntary party quotas in order to distinguish them from other types of quotas. After briefly discussing the effects of such quotas, we turn to a review of the literature that seeks to explain how current research understands those forces that impel parties to adopt quotas. This review is followed by a discussion of our contagion argument as it relates to voluntary party quotas. Beginning with our dataset of 159 countries, we searched for data on all political parties within each country. We were able to find data for 1,460 political parties in 102 countries between 1945 and 2006, and we use this to model both voluntary party quota onset and incidence. Here we isolate the critical factors—including contagion—that drive party quota adoption. We then turn to a more detailed discussion of the Swedish case and show the critical importance of contagion in explaining voluntary party quota incidence in Sweden.

Defining Voluntary Party Quotas

Gender scholars differentiate among three specific types of gender quotas—reserved-seat quotas, compulsory party quotas, and voluntary party quotas. Reserved-seat quotas set aside a certain percentage or number of legislative seats for female legislators. Compulsory party quotas require political parties to nominate a certain percentage of women for office (Tripp and Kang 2008). These quotas are required by electoral legislation or, in some cases, by the constitution.

Unlike compulsory quotas, voluntary party quotas are adopted willingly by parties and are not required by national law. They are similar to compulsory quotas because they establish some threshold for the nomination of female candidates for office; however, parties are not compelled by law to implement them. Of the different gender quotas, voluntary party quotas are by far the most common. In our data covering the period 1945–2006, we found ninety-eight parties with voluntary quotas in forty-six different countries.

The particulars of a voluntary party quota can vary in a number of ways. Typically, a quota reserves a specified number of a party's nominations for legislative office exclusively for women. Often, this is implemented as a percentage of party nominations. For example, the Flemish Green Party in the Netherlands adopted a 50 percent quota for women on its party lists at the time of the party's formation, in 1982 (Meier 2004). The size of the quota, however, can vary substantially among parties. The Flemish Social Democrats in the Netherlands eventually adopted a 25 percent quota in 1992 (Meier 2004). In single-member district systems, a voluntary party quota often determines the number of female candidates the party must nominate. For example, in Zimbabwe, the Zimbabwe African National Union-Patriotic Front (ZANU-PF) requires that women represent the party in at least thirty constituencies in the lower house election (Gaidzanwa 2004).

There are also variations in the rules that govern the formation of party lists among many parties that adopt party quotas. Parties such as the Flemish Green Party and the Swedish Democratic Labor Party require that their lists alternate between male and female candidates. This prevents parties from stacking their male candidates at the top of the list and relegating female candidates to the bottom of the list. The African National Congress requires that a woman occupy at least every third position.

Freidnevall (2003) points out that a voluntary quota is just one of several different options a party may select to increase women's representation. Parties can opt to simply spout rhetoric that embraces gender equality but avoid actually implementing policies to accomplish these goals (Lovenduski and Norris 1993). Setting as a party goal an increase in women's participation is an example of this type of device. Parties may also establish targets for women's participation, often establishing a specific time frame for increasing female representation. In addition, parties may adopt some sort of policy designed to increase women's presence within the party, such as quotas for internal party committees or increased support for women's organizations within the party. Such strategies can increase the number of women in the top echelons of the party organizations, which, in turn, can increase women's ability to run for office or improve the prospects of other women who are interested in running for office. While the use of these strategies may indicate a willingness of parties to address the position of women in the party, they often have less dramatic impacts on women's candidacy than do voluntary party quotas.

The Effect of Voluntary Party Quotas

Do voluntary party quotas increase women's legislative representation? This is a difficult question to answer on the basis of the current literature, since many authors conflate voluntary and compulsory party quotas (e.g., Reynolds 1999; Tripp and Kang 2008). For example, Tripp and Kang (2008) use one variable that does not differentiate between voluntary and compulsory party quotas in their empirical analysis. This is problematic, given that, in systems with compulsory party quotas, all parties must use quotas, whereas there is no such requirement in systems with voluntary quotas. Tripp and Kang, however, note that their models that used only voluntary quotas, which were not presented, did demonstrate a positive correlation between the presence of voluntary party quotas and women's representation.

In chapter 2, we showed that the percentage of women in the legislature was influenced by the number of parties with voluntary party quotas. As the number of parties with quotas increased, so did the percentage of women in the legislature. From our own work, it appears that the presence of quotas positively impacts women's representation and that that effect increases as more parties adopt quotas. Yet, we found some contradictory effects on the incidence of female chief executives.

Adopting Quotas

Given the impact of voluntary party quotas on women's representation, it is critical to understand the processes that drive parties to employ them. The existing research focuses on factors that are similar to those found in the broader literature on women's representation—namely women's political mobilization and the electoral system. Yet, the existing research also focuses on party characteristics, such as ideology. In addition, parties have been found to make decisions on the basis of their contexts. Competitive pressures can lead to a diffusion of voluntary party quotas systemwide as parties respond to the adoption of quotas by their competitors.

Greater levels of women's political mobilization are often cited as key factors that determine the level of women's political representation. In the literature on legislative representation, scholars find a positive correlation between female labor force participation and the percentage of women in the legislature (Matland 1998; Norris 1985; Rule 1987; Salmond 2006). Labor force participation serves as a proxy for women's political mobilization in these arguments. As the number of women in the labor force increases, the political demands made by women are also thought to increase. Not only does participation raise consciousness, leading to greater desire for change; it also provides women with resources, making it easier for them to organize politically. As more women become politically active, the demands, in this case for legislative representation, should increase, as well.

Research on the adoption of voluntary party quotas highlights the critical role played by women's political mobilization (Caul 2001; Krook 2006a, 2006b, 2007a, 2009). The more women mobilize and push for their political inclusion, the more they are likely to win acceptance of policies that increase their representation. Kolinsky (1991) argues that changes in women's voting patterns in the 1970s spurred the adoption of quotas by German political parties. Female voters began to shift their support away from the conservative Christian Democratic Union and Christian Social Union and moved toward left-leaning parties, such as the Social Democratic Party, which were more supportive of gender equity. Thus, as women became more conscious of their political interests, they shifted their vote toward parties that supported those interests. This shift also increased women's membership in these parties, increasing their influence within the party and making it easier to push for policies to promote equality, such as voluntary party quotas (Kolinsky 1991).

Political mobilization by women within parties is also essential. Freidnevall, Dahlerup, and Skjeie (2006) argue that the high level of women's representation in the Nordic countries is partly explained by the long history of effective women's organizations within political parties. Similarly, the adoption of party quotas by the Socialist Workers Party and the Communist Party in Spain and by the African National Congress in South Africa occurred only after successful organization and mobilization by women within their respective parties (Myakayaka-Manzini 2003; Verge 2009). Thus, the push for quotas is stronger in parties where women are able to obtain critical leadership positions (Dahlerup 1988; Kolinsky 1991).

The broader literature on women's representation often focuses on the effects of electoral systems. As we discussed previously, there is strong evidence that women's representation is greater in proportional-representation systems where higher district magnitudes increase opportunities for women in legislatures (Darcy, Welch, and Clark 1994; Kenworthy and Malami 1999; Lakeman 1976; Matland 1993, 1998; Matland and Studlar 1996; Norris 1985; Reynolds 1999; Rule 1987; Salmond 2006). In these systems, parties face a lower risk from nominating female candidates than do parties in single-member district systems, for example. If the potential costs of nominating women are lower in high-district-magnitude proportional-representation systems, then it is possible that the potential costs of adopting a voluntary party quota to increase women's representation will also be lower. In addition, since these systems tend to produce a greater number of parties, we may find more intense competitive pressures among these parties that can spur quota adoption by parties seeking to capture female voters. Since these systems tend to produce more parties, they also produce more opportunities for left-wing parties, which have been shown to be more likely to adopt quotas. Yet, existing research on the adoption of voluntary party quotas has found little evidence that electoral systems matter (Caul 2001; Kittilson 2006).

Parties may also adopt quotas because of their ideological commitments to gender equality and fairness. Parties that are more committed to women's political equality are more likely to adopt voluntary quotas. Perhaps not surprisingly, this normative preference for equality is used to explain why leftist political parties appear more likely to support women's issues and women's political representation (Caul 2001; Jenson 1982; Kolinsky 1991; Krook 2006a, 2006b, 2007a, 2009; Lovenduski and Norris 1993). Left-leaning parties are simply more willing to see gender equality as a goal that should be achieved with something like a quota. For other parties, especially those on the right, quotas may appear to be discriminatory, since they are thought to undermine opportunities for qualified male candidates. Previous work on quota adoption finds that leftist parties are more likely to adopt quotas, as well (Caul 2001; Kittilson 2006).

The ideological association between left-wing parties and gender equality may have waned over time. Matland and Studlar (1996) argue that differences between leftist and other parties in terms of gender equality may be less salient than in the past. This may signal that the commitment to gender equality has become more broadly accepted. Krook (2009) argues that many governments responded favorably to the Platform for Action produced by the UN's Fourth World Conference on Women, held in Beijing in 1995. This may signal a broader acceptance of gender equality that could make left-wing parties less distinctive.

Contagion and Voluntary Party Quota Adoption

Should we expect contagion to impact the adoption of voluntary party quotas? The existing research on the adoption of quotas has not found a relationship between women's legislative representation and the adoption of party quotas (Caul 2001). Yet, there are reasons to believe that women's representation may spur voluntary party quota adoption. As women increase their representation in a legislature, this may signal their increasing influence in their parties. Thus, the election of more women legislators may mean that parties will come under greater pressure to adopt quotas. In addition, as women win more seats, it may reduce parties' fears of quota adoption. It suggests that a party's vote total may not suffer as women are accommodated. Some parties may see the growth in the number of female representatives as an indication that the nomination of women may actually increase their vote share.

The competition among political parties may also induce quota adoption in ways in line with our contagion argument. Matland and Studlar (1996) argue that the decision by a party to nominate female candidates may lead other parties to do the same in order to attract female voters. In some cases, the nomination of female candidates by small parties not only indicates that the nomination of candidates may not cost votes but also increases the pressure on other parties to do the same (Matland and Studlar 1996). Thus, competition for female voters may spur parties to nominate female candidates.

This same logic applies to the adoption of voluntary party quotas. Once one party adopts a gender quota, others may feel compelled to follow suit in order to remain competitive (Caul 2001; Meier 2004). The adoption of quotas by left-wing parties in Spain eventually spread to nationalist parties (Verge 2009). The Social Democratic Party in Sweden adopted quotas only after they were adopted by smaller, more extreme left-wing parties (Freidnevall 2003). Meier (2004) observed a similar process in Belgium.

Competition may, however, not lead to diffusion. Some researchers argue that uncertainty over electoral outcomes prevents parties from adopting quotas (Murray 2004; Randall 1982; Stevenson 2000). The decision to adopt a gender quota may turn off those voters, especially on the right, who see quotas as a violation of equality. Parties that are unsure of the extent to which they will increase their vote share by adopting a quota may resist the effort. This uncertainty, however, may lessen as other parties adopt similar quotas without undermining their vote shares.

The Distribution of Voluntary Party Quotas

To understand why parties adopt voluntary quotas, we created a cross-sectional time-series dataset of 1,460 political parties in 102 countries between 1945 and 2006. Of these parties, we have ninety-six parties that adopted a voluntary party quota during this period.

Figure 5.1 graphs the adoption of voluntary party quotas in our sample by year from the year of our first recorded adoption, 1971, through the end our sample, 2006. The figure reveals that the adoption of party quotas began slowly in the 1970s. The pace of adoptions picked up significantly in the 1980s and 1990s before slowing after 2002.

While the pace of adoption slowed in the beginning of the twenty-first century, the number of parties with quotas reached its height during this

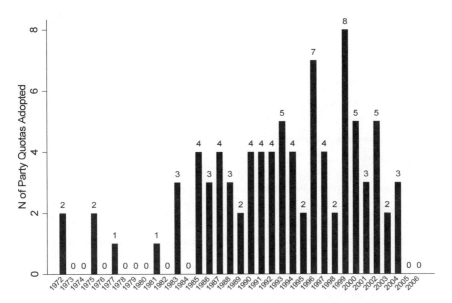

Fig. 5.1. Voluntary Party Quotas Adopted by Year

period. Figure 5.2 presents the number of voluntary party quotas in our sample by year.

Parties with voluntary quotas are not randomly distributed across the globe. Figure 5.3 presents the regional breakdown of parties with quotas between 1971 and 2006. The pattern shows that voluntary party quotas are predominantly a European phenomenon. The first parties to adopt quotas were the Liberal Party in Sweden and the Liberal Left Party in Norway in 1972. The first non-European party to adopt a quota in our sample was the Workers' Party (Partido dos Trabalhadores) in Brazil in 1986. Even in 2006, European parties accounted for 63.4 percent of our sample. This fits with Dahlerup's (2006) argument that European countries, in particular Nordic countries, adopted party quotas as part of an "incremental strategy" toward achieving gender parity. The regional distribution also suggests that party quotas may be associated with countries with higher levels of development and longer periods of democracy, given the prevalence of quotas in advanced, industrialized democracies in northern Europe. Yet, this should not obscure the fact that parties in Latin America, Asia, and Africa also adopted quotas in more recent years.

Modeling Voluntary Party Quota Selection

In order to help determine the reasons parties adopted voluntary quotas, we implement two strategies to model voluntary party selection. First, we conduct survival analysis of the data to model time to the onset of a voluntary quota by a party. This analysis allows us to better understand those factors that explain the adoption of the initial voluntary quotas, since we are analyzing time to adoption. Second, we analyze the incidence of voluntary party quotas. Put another way, we isolate those factors that explain why a party employs a voluntary quota in a given year.

The Onset of Voluntary Party Quotas

The dataset is organized in a cross-sectional time-series format with the individual political parties as the panels and time measured by year. We include only those years during which the party's country was considered a democracy. Parties enter the analysis according to their year of foundation. If the year was prior to 1945, we entered the party in 1945. For those parties where we do not have a founding date, we entered them in the year of their first election. Parties exit, or "fail," the year they adopt a voluntary party quota. Parties that do not adopt a quota exit the year of their final election. Unlike

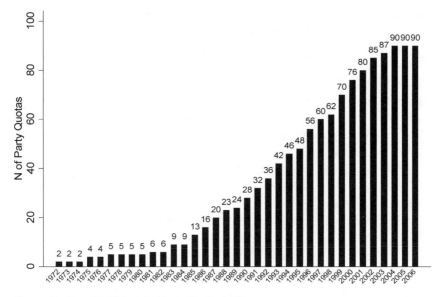

Fig. 5.2. Parties with Voluntary Party Quotas by Year

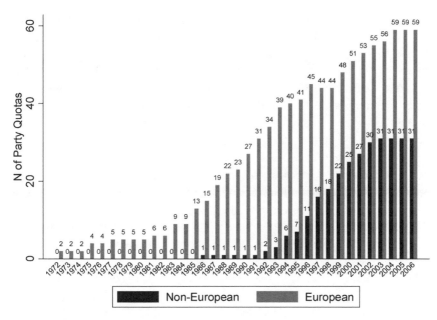

Fig. 5.3. Voluntary Party Quotas by Region and Year

the election of a female executive (see chapter 3), the adoption of voluntary party quotas is not a repeated event.

We use a Cox proportional-hazards model to estimate the time to adoption of voluntary party quotas. We ran tests to ensure that we do not violate the proportional-hazards assumption. When the tests indicated a violation of the assumption, we included an interaction between the offending variable and time (Box-Steffensmeier and Jones 2003). We calculated robust standard errors clustered on individual political parties to deal with potential heteroscedasticity.[2] We used the Breslow method to deal with ties.

We include several variables to measure the impact of country-level social and economic factors on the adoption of voluntary party quotas. First, all parties were coded with their country's percentage of female labor force participation (Salmond 2006; World Bank 2006). Parties may be more likely to adopt quotas if women's political activism is significant. Second, we include GDP per capita in constant U.S. dollars (World Bank 2009). This variable controls for any differences between more and less developed countries. Finally, we include a variable that measures years since suffrage.

The existing literature argues that left-wing parties are more likely to adopt quotas than other parties, depending on their particular ideological positions. To control for this, we include a dummy variable for left-wing parties. We coded all parties that represent themselves as being left-wing, socialist, social democratic, green, or environmentalist.[3] Given the subjective nature of this determination, we allowed the parties to define themselves. This may be problematic for several reasons. There are significant differences among countries on the standard left-right ideological scale. In addition, though a party may embrace social democratic rhetoric, it may not actually represent such positions. One potential solution would be to use data from the Comparative Manifestos Project (Budge et al. 2001; Klingeman et al. 2006) or another source. The problem, of course, is that we lack comparable scales across all countries in our sample. Consequently, we use our imperfect measure of party ideology.

Previous research has found that electoral systems have little impact on quota adoption. However, given the importance of the variable thus far in our own research and the differences between our models and those of other scholars, we include a measure of district magnitude to control for its potential impact (Beck et al. 2001; Golder 2005; Johnson and Wallack 2008).

As we discussed earlier, there is a clear regional bias in the distribution of voluntary party quotas. Thus, we include a series of regional dummy variables to control for regional effects.

Parties may adopt quotas for strategic reasons in order to better position themselves in their electoral competition. We include a variable to deal with the potential strategic adoption of quotas—a measure of the party's vote percentage or its coalition vote percentage in the most recent election. This variable may also shed light on whether smaller parties are more likely than larger ones to adopt quotas.

To measure contagion, we include four variables. First, we include the percentage of women in the legislature (Inter-Parliamentary Union 2008a, 2008b). The inclusion of women in the legislature should increase women's political influence. If this is so, it could impact the adoption of quotas. Second, we include a dummy variable indicating whether the chief executive is a woman (Gleditsch and Chiozza 2009; Worldwide Guide to Women in Leadership 2009). Third, we include a measure of the number of parties in the country that already use quotas. Previous research suggests that quotas are more likely to be adopted if other parties do the same. Finally, parties may adopt voluntary quotas in response to the existence of a compulsory party quota (Meier 2004). To control for this possibility, we include a dummy variable indicating whether the country employed a compulsory party quota in the given year.

Table 5.1 presents the result of our event history model. We report the hazard ratios, rather than the coefficients. The hazard ratio is simply the

Table 5.1. Results of Cox Proportional Hazards Model

Variables	Model 1	
	Hazard Ratio	Standard Error
Natural Log of GDP per Capita Constant U.S.$	1.171	0.168
Female Labor Force Participation	0.992	0.011
Years since Suffrage	1.000	0.007
Natural Log of District Magnitude	1.162	0.111
Left Party	6.648***	1.666
Vote Percentage	11.586***	6.152
N Party Quotas	1.177*	0.115
Compulsory Party Quota	1.919*	0.699
Female Executive in Year	0.905	0.359
Percent Women in the Legislature	1.041**	0.019
South and Central America	0.612	0.232
North America	0.216	0.225
Africa and the Middle East	0.652	0.274
Asia	0.082**	0.081
Observations	12224	
Number of Parties	1287	
X²	144.00***	

*p < 0.10, ** p < 0.05, *** p < 0.01

exponentiated coefficient of each variable. This allows us to determine how a one-unit increase in the independent variable affects the hazard or the likelihood of a party adopting a quota. If we examine the results, we find several factors that explain the adoption of voluntary party quotas. First, economic and cultural factors appear to have little impact on the adoption of voluntary party quotas. The GDP per capita variable is statistically insignificant. None of the other variables that measure economic and cultural factors—labor force participation and decades since suffrage—had an effect on the hazard of voluntary party quota adoption.

The electoral system does not appear to affect independently the hazard of quota adoption. The district magnitude variable is not statistically significant, though it is correlated with quota adoption. This replicates earlier findings. The left-wing party dummy variable is strongly correlated with voluntary quota adoption. The variable is statistically significant, and the odds ratio is quite large. On the basis of the results of Model 1, we conclude that being a left-wing party increases the hazard by more than 500 percent. We can see the impact more clearly in Figure 5.4, which presents the cumulative hazard of party adoption for both left-wing and nonleft-wing parties. The difference between left-wing and other parties is quite large. The graph of the cumulative hazard does show, however, that the hazard of voluntary party quota adoption by nonleft-wing parties increases over time.

Previous studies suggest that parties may adopt party quotas for strategic reasons. We find strong evidence of this. Some researchers suggest that larger parties are more likely to adopt quotas after smaller parties do the same. The results, however, do not support this. On the basis of the results of Model 1, we find that increasing the average of the vote percentage variable by one standard deviation increases the hazard of voluntary party quota adoption by 46 percent. Thus, there is little evidence that small parties are early adopters of voluntary party quotas. The vote percent variable showed strong indications of having a nonproportional hazard; therefore, we included an interaction between it and time. The interaction term is positively correlated and statistically significant. Thus, as time passes, the impact of vote percent accelerates, increasing the hazard of quota adoption.

What about contagion? On the one hand, the presence of a female chief executive does not spur parties to adopt voluntary quotas. On the other hand, the level of women's legislative representation does impact the adoption of voluntary party quotas. The percentage women in the legislature variable is statistically significant and positively correlated with the onset of voluntary party quotas. An increase of one standard deviation in the percentage

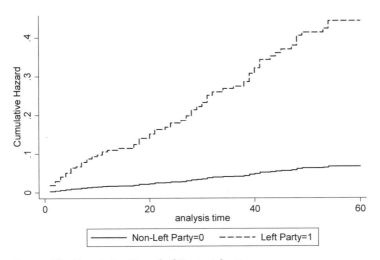

Fig. 5.4. The Cumulative Hazard of Quota Adoption

women in the legislature variable increases the hazard of voluntary quota adoption by 38.6 percent. This is an important finding, since it indicates that, while party quotas may increase female representation, increasing levels of female representation in the legislature increases the likelihood of parties to adopt quotas.

Similarly, the existence of compulsory party quotas has a positive impact on the adoption of voluntary party quotas. If a country has a compulsory party quota, the hazard of voluntary party adoption increases by 91.8 percent. Thus, parties respond to national-level institutional changes that encourage women's representation by adopting similar rules. In addition, parties do appear to take into account the decisions of other parties about quotas. If one additional party in a system adopts a quota, the hazard of party quota adoption increases by 17.7 percent. Parties, therefore, are clearly impacted by the decisions of other parties. This is strong, important evidence demonstrating that women's representation is contagious.

The regional dummy variables demonstrate a predictable pattern. The reference group is the European dummy; therefore, the hazard ratios represent the effect of the region in comparison to European countries. All of the hazards of the regional dummy variables show that parties in these regions are less likely than parties in European regions to adopt voluntary party quotas. However, for only two of them—Asia and North America—are the findings statistically significant.

The Incidence of Voluntary Party Quotas

Our event history analysis demonstrated those factors that explain the onset of quotas. We now turn to an analysis of the incidence of quotas. This analysis strives to understand those factors that explain why a party has a voluntary party quota in a given year. In our sample, only 8 percent of observations contain a voluntary party quota. Thus, we use Tomz, King, and Zeng's (2000) logit model that corrects for rare events. We calculate robust standard errors clustered on individual political parties to deal with the fact that the model errors may be correlated by party. The dependent variable, therefore, simply indicates whether the party featured a quota in a given year. For the most part, we use the same covariates for our logit model that we used in our previous Cox model. We include but do not report a series of decade dummy variables to control for time periods.

Table 5.2 presents the results of our rare events logit model of voluntary party quota incidence. In terms of economic and cultural factors, we find limited evidence of their impact. The wealth variable, the natural log of GDP per capita, is positively correlated with quota adoption, and the correlation is statistically significant. If we increase the GDP per capita variable from one standard deviation below to one standard deviation above the average,

Table 5.2. Rare Event Logit Model of Voluntary Party Quotas

Variables	Model 2	
	Coefficient	Standard Error
Natural Log of GDP per Capita Constant U.S. $	0.428***	0.147
Female Labor Force Participation	0.002	0.013
Years since Suffrage	−0.001	0.007
Natural Log of District Magnitude	0.171	0.119
Left Party	2.358***	0.337
Vote Percentage$_{t-1}$	3.208***	0.652
N Party Quotas$_{t-1}$	0.324***	0.102
Compulsory Party Quota	0.529*	0.315
Female Executive in Year$_{t-1}$	−0.334	0.368
Percent Women in the Legislature$_{t-1}$	0.042**	0.018
South and Central America	−0.488	0.520
North America	1.577	1.120
Africa and the Middle East	−0.221	0.506
Asia	−2.262**	0.960
Constant	10.826***	1.705
Observations	12579	
Number of Parties	1055	
X^2	190.00***	

* $p < 0.10$, ** $p < 0.05$, *** $p < 0.01$

the probability of voluntary quota party incidence increases by 2.2 percent. This supports the argument that voluntary party quotas are more likely to occur in wealthier countries. Neither the labor force participation nor the years since suffrage variable is statistically significant, suggesting that neither has an independent effect on the probability of quota incidence.

The district magnitude variable is positively correlated with the incidence of voluntary party quotas; however, it is not statistically significant. Thus, we find that electoral institutions have no independent impact on the likelihood of a voluntary party quota.

Party ideology clearly matters. Our left-wing party dummy variable is positively correlated with voluntary party quota incidence, and the correlation is statistically significant. If we increase the value of the left party variable from 0 to 1, the probability of the existence of a party quota increases by 7.2 percent. This mirrors our previous results, as well as the work of other scholars, which found the link between left parties and party quotas.

Vote percentage matters. Increasing the vote percentage variable from one standard deviation below to one above the average boosts the probability of quota incidence by 1.8 percent. Thus, again we find evidence that larger parties are more likely to use quotas than are smaller parties.

Our model of voluntary party quota incidence finds evidence of contagion, as well. We also find that the adoption of quotas by other parties increases the likelihood that a party will use a voluntary gender quota. The number of quota parties variable is statistically significant and positively correlated with voluntary gender quota incidence. Figure 5.5 graphs the predicted probability of quota incidence for the number of party quotas.[4] The results show that, as the number of other parties in the system increases, so does the probability that a party will have a voluntary quota, as well.

Other measures of contagion show mixed results. The female executive variable is statistically insignificant. Thus, we find no evidence that women's representation in the executive affects the incidence of voluntary party quotas. Yet, we do find evidence that the percentage of women in the legislature matters. If we shift the value of the percentage women in the legislature variable from one standard deviation below its mean to one standard deviation above its mean, we increase the probability of a voluntary party quota by 1.4 percent. Additionally, the presence of a compulsory party quota also influences party decisions on voluntary quotas. The national quota variable is statistically significant and positively correlated with the incidence of voluntary party quotas. A national quota increases the probability of a party quota by 1.1 percent. Consequently, national commitments to gender equality can impact individual party decisions.

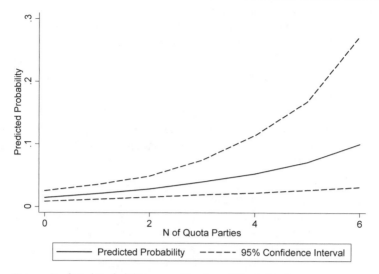

Fig. 5.5. Predicted Probabilities over Number of Quota Parties

We find that regional differences have limited impact. The reference category in our models is European countries. With the exception of Asia, parties in no other region are more or less likely to feature voluntary party quotas than are European parties. The Asia dummy variable, however, is statistically significant and negatively correlated with the incidence of voluntary party quota adoption. The probability that a party in Asia will feature a party quota is 2.2 percent lower than that for parties in Europe.

Discussion of Results

Our statistical analysis of voluntary party quota onset and incidence identified several key factors that explain why some parties use quotas and others avoid them. There appears to be little evidence that economic and social factors matter. Neither years since universal suffrage nor women's labor force participation impacts either quota onset or incidence. We found some evidence that wealth matters for quota incidence, but it does not seem to explain onset. Thus, we have weak support for broader social and economic factors as independent causes of quota employment by parties.

We also found no evidence that electoral system differences independently impact the use of voluntary quotas by parties. In both sets of results, we found a positive correlation between district magnitude and the onset or incidence of a voluntary party quota. Yet, the variable is not statistically significant in either multivariate model. We cannot, therefore, conclude that the electoral system is an independent determinant of quotas.

Ideology is a consistent, strong predictor of voluntary party quota use. Our results showed that left-wing parties were more likely to employ quotas than were other parties, and this effect was quite substantively significant. This highlights the important link between the ideological position of parties and their behavior in the area of gender equality. We do see evidence in the onset model that, over time, the hazard for nonleft-wing parties to adopt a quota (see Figure 5.4) did increase. Yet, the change was minimal. The results presented here clearly demonstrate the impact of left-wing ideology on party decisions concerning quotas.

We did find evidence that voluntary party quota adoption is correlated with the vote percentage of parties. As vote percentage increases, we found both a greater hazard of quota onset and a larger probability of quota incidence. Thus, we find that larger parties are more likely to adopt gender quotas. This runs counter to the prevailing wisdom that smaller parties are more likely to be early adopters. Larger parties adopt quotas later in order to protect themselves.[5] Our results may reflect the fact that we included in our dataset all parties in each election for which we could obtain electoral data and did not limit ourselves to major parties that met an arbitrary vote threshold.

In both models, we found evidence that parties influence each other. The number of parties in the system with a voluntary party quota encouraged both onset and incidence of voluntary party quotas. This finding resonates with previous research, which argues that parties behave strategically and use gender quotas to remain competitive.

The existence of a compulsory party quota influenced parties, as well. We found evidence that the existence of compulsory party quotas was correlated with both the onset and the incidence of voluntary party quotas. As Meier (2004) points out, some observers might expect that the existence of a compulsory party quota obviates the need for a voluntary one; however, parties in Belgium adopted voluntary quotas after a mandatory one. The results may simply reflect the fact that, once a mandatory quota is in place, parties have a stronger incentive to adopt voluntary ones, since their potential costs are minimized—the parties must use a gender quota of some sort regardless of their ideological leanings or other concerns. The result does, however, further demonstrate that a commitment to women's representation in one area, in this case a national compulsory quota, can spark change in another.

We did find some other evidence of contagion. The presence of a female executive appears to have no impact on the adoption of voluntary party quotas, however. In both models, the variable is statistically insignificant. This finding may reflect the simple fact that female executives are quite rare; therefore, their impact is quite limited. The percentage of women in the legislature clearly matters. The percentage of female legislators is correlated with both the onset and the incidence of voluntary party quotas. The magnitude of the effect does appear to differ, however, for onset and incidence. The effect of the percentage women in the legislature variable is quite strong, meaning that, as the percentage increases, the time to quota onset falls quickly. This most likely reflects the fact that most early quota adopters were in European countries, many of which had significant rates of women's participation earlier than other regions. The percentage of women in the legislature is correlated with the incidence of quotas; however, the magnitude of the effect is smaller. Again, this may be a result of the difference in the question each model is answering. To further understand the impact of these factors, we examine their influence in the case of Sweden.

The Impact of Contagion in Sweden

Our results suggest that, in terms of voluntary party quotas, contagion manifests itself in two ways—the level of women's legislative representation and the number of other parties in the system with quotas. To further tease out just how powerful the effects of contagion are, we examine the Swedish case. In terms of voluntary party quotas, Sweden is interesting for several reasons. First, in terms of the remaining variables from our statistical models, Sweden ranks near the top in all of our key independent variables. Table 5.3 compares Sweden and the rest of Europe on values of our main variables. In our data, Sweden is, on average, wealthier, features a greater level of women in the labor force, adopted universal suffrage earlier, and has a greater district magnitude than other European countries. Only the wealth variable was shown to be statistically significant in our incidence model; nonetheless, the differences with Europe suggest that Sweden should have a more favorable atmosphere for gender equality than your average European country.

Table 5.3. Comparing Sweden to Europe

Variables	Sweden	Europe	Difference	P Value
Avg. GDP Per Capita	$20,422.39	$13,067.22	$7,355.17	0.000
Avg. Female Labor Force Participation	71.6%	56.7%	14.8%	0.000
Avg. Year of Universal Suffrage	56.5	49.9	6.6	0.000
Avg. Log of District Magnitude	2.4	2.1	0.03	0.049

Note: P-values are from a difference in mean t-test.

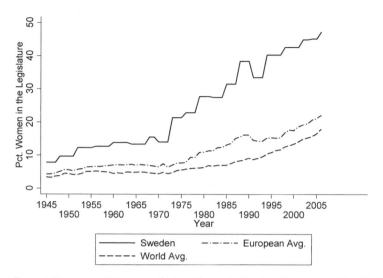

Fig. 5.6. Percentage Women in the Legislature in Sweden, Europe, and the World

Second, the Swedish parliament, the Riksdag, has a strong record of women's representation. Figure 5.6 plots the global and the European yearly averages for percentage of women in the legislature as well as the percentage for Sweden. The data series clearly show that Sweden has elected more women than the average European or global democracy in every year between 1945 and 2006. If contagion matters, then this high level of women in the legislature should push parties toward quotas.

Finally, while Sweden has not adopted a compulsory party quota or reserved seats, many Swedish political parties have adopted voluntary party quotas. By 1993, five Swedish political parties had adopted voluntary party quotas: the Liberal Party in 1972, the Green Party in 1987, the former communist Left Party in 1987, the Christian Democrats in 1987, and the Swedish Democratic Labor Party in 1993. Of Sweden's major parties, only the Conservative Party remained without a gender quota by 2006. What explains this commitment to quotas in Sweden? The existing research points to the important role played by ideology. In fact, the failure of the Conservative Party to adopt a voluntary quota reflects its ideological position that quotas represent an undemocratic mechanism that increases the opportunities for women at the expense of male candidates (Diaz 2005; Freidnevall 2003; Krook 2009; Wangnerud 2005). Another critical factor that explains the number of Swedish parties with voluntary quotas is the competition for voters that is created by such quotas. The need to compete with other parties that had already adopted quotas compelled most of the remaining Swedish parties to adopt them (Freidnevall 2003). This is particularly true for left-leaning parties in Sweden. The adoption of a voluntary party quota by the Green Party in 1981 and the Left Party in 1987 pushed the larger Swedish Democratic Labor Party to adopt one in 1993. The fear of losing voters to other left-wing parties, in part, drove this decision (Freidnevall 2003).

We utilize our empirical results presented earlier to demonstrate how contagion could impact the adoption of voluntary party quotas in Sweden. We begin by examining the impact of the level of women's legislative representation. Using the results of our rare events logit Model 2 from Table 5.2, we estimate the marginal effect of the percentage of women in the legislature variable equal to the annual world average. Thus, we can simulate the magnitude by which the probability of adopting a quota would decrease if the Riksdag contained the global average percentage of women in the legislature, rather than the actual value. We estimate marginal effects for an average Swedish party, meaning that we set all other variables at their yearly averages. We use simulated coefficients to estimate the marginal effect of reducing the yearly Swedish percentage of women in the Riksdag to the yearly average percentage of women in the world's legislatures in our sample.

Figure 5.7 graphs the predicted marginal effect described earlier. The solid line plots the marginal effect of the percentage women in the legislature variable set to zero. The gray bars around this solid line represent the 95 percent confidence interval around our prediction. The predicted marginal effect is statistically significant for every year. The marginal effect is always negative, meaning that reducing the level of women's representation in Sweden lowers the probability of voluntary quota adoption. Initially, the marginal effect is quite small. Yet, by 1986, the marginal effect is below −10 percent, and by 1989 it is below −20 percent. The average drop in the probability across all years is 11.8 percent. These predicted, simulated results clearly demonstrate the contagious effect of women's legislative representation.

We can use a similar method to estimate the impact of contagion through voluntary party quota adoption in Sweden. Again, using the results from Model 2 in Table 5.2, we estimate the marginal effect of the number of quota parties variable set to zero. Consequently, the simulated marginal effect attempts to measure the reduction in the probability of quota adoption if Sweden featured no parties with a quota. Again, we set all other variables to their yearly averages to measure the marginal effect for an average political party in Sweden.

Figure 5.8 presents the results of our simulation. Again, the solid line plots the marginal effect of quota adoption for an average Swedish party in

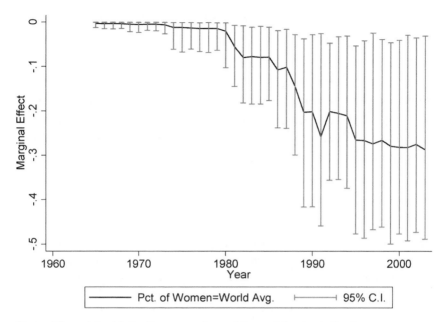

Fig. 5.7. Women's Legislative Representation and Quota Adoption in Sweden

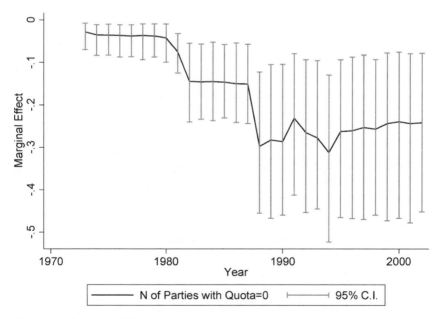

Fig. 5.8. The Presence of Quota Parties and Quota Adoption in Sweden

a given year. The gray bars around this solid line represent the 95 percent confidence interval around our prediction. The simulated results all proved to be statistically significant, as well. The results show the strong impact that competitive pressures had on spurring voluntary quota adoption in Sweden. As the number of parties with quotas increases, so does the magnitude of the marginal effect. In 1994, five parties employed quotas. From 1994 to the end of our sample in 2006, the marginal effect of reducing the number of party quotas variable drops by more than 24 percent for every year. On average, the marginal effect of zero parties is −17.5 for the whole period examined here.

Conclusion

The adoption and use of a voluntary quota represents a strong commitment by a party to increasing women's representation. We analyzed statistically both the onset and the incidence of voluntary party quotas to determine which factors best explain their adoption and use. We found several important factors that explain the use of a voluntary party quota. Wealth seems to play a role, since we found evidence that parties in wealthier countries were more likely to adopt quotas. We also found that left-leaning parties, as predicted by other scholars, are indeed more likely to adopt quotas. We found that, as vote totals increased, the probability of quota incidence increased and the time to onset decreased, suggesting that larger parties are more likely to adopt quotas than smaller ones.

In particular, we wanted to test whether our arguments about contagion mattered. Our results are broadly consistent with the notion that representation in one area or institution impacts women's representation in others. In the case of onset and incidence of voluntary party quotas, we found strong evidence that the level of women's legislative representation affects both the timing and the use of voluntary party quotas in our cross-national analysis. As the percentage of women in the legislature increased, the time to the adoption of a voluntary quota decreased and the probability of incidence increased.

We also found evidence of contagion through competitive pressures. As other parties adopted voluntary party quotas, the remaining parties felt a competitive pressure to do the same. In our statistical models, we found evidence that parties adopted quotas more quickly and used them more frequently as the number of other parties with quotas increased. This is an important finding, for it shows that contagion is a multifaceted process.

The presence of a compulsory party quota increased the likelihood of voluntary party quotas, as well. Thus, a national commitment to greater women's equality in the legislature pushed parties to adopt quotas. This is an important finding for our contagion argument, for it shows how decisions at one level, in this case the nation, impact the decisions of actors at another level, in this case the party level.

6

Contagion and the Adoption of National Quotas

In 2000, the warring factions in Burundi's civil war signed a peace agreement in Arusha, Tanzania. The Arusha Accord ended a nearly decade-long civil war in which thousands of people died and many more thousands were displaced. Peace led to the writing of a new constitution, which was approved by referendum in February 2005. Article 164 of the new constitution erected a 30 percent reserved-seat quota for women in parliament (International Institute for Democracy and Electoral Assistance and Stockholm University 2006). The quota law substantially increased women's representation in Burundi, increasing the representation of women in the legislature from 18.4 percent in 2004 to 30.5 percent in 2005 (Inter-Parliamentary Union 2011).

In 1999, Costa Rica adopted a compulsory party quota that required all parties to nominate women for 40 percent of the "electable positions" on party lists (International Institute for Democracy and Electoral Assistance and Stockholm University 2006). Electable positions were those positions in which a party had won a seat in the previous elections. Thus, female candidates were not simply tacked on to the bottom of the party list. The application of the quota appears to have worked. The percentage of women in the legislature in Costa Rica grew from 19.3 percent in 2001 to 35.1 percent in 2002 (Inter-Parliamentary Union 2011).

The adoption of these national quotas in both Costa Rica and Burundi raises an important question: given quotas' powerful positive effect on women's legislative representation, why have other countries not adopted them?[1] In this chapter, we attempt to answer this question by undertaking a statistical analysis of national quota onset and incidence. Our results clearly indicate that contagion significantly impacts the onset and incidence of national quotas. The effect of women in the legislature or the presence of a female executive has different effects on different types of quotas. Moreover, we show strong evidence that regional policy diffusion plays an important role in explaining quota adoption.

Besides contagion, our analysis exposes several other key factors that explain the presence of national quotas. Our results highlight important differences in the factors that lead to the adoption of different types of national quotas. The processes that lead to the implementation of compulsory party quotas and reserved-seat quotas are not identical. This finding is critical because it demonstrates the importance of avoiding the temptation to treat different types of quotas as identical institutions without noting important differences between them. In addition, our results clearly support the view that national quotas are a fast-track approach to gender equity (Dahlerup 2005; Norris 2006). Our analysis shows that national quotas are less likely to be adopted in wealthy, institutionalized democracies with strong records of women's legislative representation than in countries without these traditions. Instead, they are adopted by countries as a way to overcome the gender gap quickly, without waiting for the traditional processes that have increased women's representation in more developed democracies such as the Nordic countries.

We start by defining national quotas. Here we explain the differences between our two main types of national quotas—compulsory party quotas and reserved-seat quotas. We then discuss the effects of these quotas on women's legislative representation by referencing both our previous analysis and the broader literature. At this point, we explain why we believe that contagion should influence the existence of national quotas. Our statistical analysis follows this discussion. Using a dataset of 159 countries, we model both the onset and the incidence of national quotas.

Defining National Quotas

Beyond voluntary party quotas, there are two other major types of quotas— compulsory party quotas and reserved-seat quotas. Compulsory party quotas require parties to nominate a certain percentage of female candidates in each election. They may also require other gender-equity solutions such as the placement of female candidates in certain positions on the list. For example, some quotas require that parties alternate the male and female candidates on their lists. Similarly, the size of the quota can vary quite extensively among different countries. Niger, for example, adopted a 10 percent quota in 2002, while France adopted a 50 percent quota in 2000.

Reserved-seat quotas go beyond regulating the process of candidate selection to reserving a certain portion of legislative seats for female legislators. While quotas increase the electoral opportunities for women, reserved-seat quotas affirm women's participation in the legislative process (Meier 2000). Thus, reserved-seat quotas go much farther to guarantee the presence of women in the legislature. As with compulsory party quotas, the percentage of seats reserved for women can vary. In Bangladesh, 13 percent of seats are reserved for women, while Burundi reserves 40 percent of seats.

Compulsory party and reserved-seat quotas may differ in their commitment to women's representation. They do, however, have one critical characteristic in common: they represent national attempts to deal with the inequality in women's representation. Unlike voluntary party quotas that are adopted voluntarily by individual parties, both compulsory party and reserved-seat quotas are adopted through a national political process and impact all actors in the system. Often these quotas are simply laws adopted by the legislature, but in some cases they are enshrined in the national constitution at its formation or by amendment. Compulsory party and reserved-seat quotas can have a much broader impact on women's representation than voluntary party quotas because of their broader scope. Because of this common national commitment, we refer to both of these quotas as national quotas.

The Effects of National Quotas

Do national quotas—either reserved-seat quotas or compulsory party quotas—impact women's legislative representation? The existing research consistently finds that national quotas do in fact increase women's legislative representation (Jones 2009; Tripp and Kang 2008). In addition, our empirical analysis in chapters 2 and 3 found that both compulsory seat quotas and reserved-seat quotas had a strong, positive impact of on women's legislative representation, while reserved-seat quotas were also related to executive representation. The presence of national quotas in fact had a strong, substantive impact on the percentage of women in the legislature.

Other research has found, however, that the impact of compulsory seat quotas can vary with other factors, in particular the electoral system. In Indonesia, the failure of the 30 percent compulsory party quota to elect more women is blamed on the semi-open list proportional-representation system that limited the success of female candidates (Siregar 2006). Compulsory party quotas are likely to be more effective in countries that utilize closed-list, high-district-magnitude electoral systems (Htun and Jones 2002; Norris 2004). Given that these systems generally increase women's representation by lowering the costs of party nominations of women, it is not surprising that they may amplify the effects of compulsory party quotas. While compulsory party quotas are national quotas that may represent a broader commitment to gender equity than, say, voluntary party quotas, it is not always true that the quotas have a significant impact if, for example, they are weakly enforced. Several scholars note that such quotas are often not strongly enforced, allowing parties to avoid reaching the required quota for female candidates (Htun and Jones 2002; Norris 2004; Schwindt-Bayer 2009). Brazil, for instance, maintains a compulsory party quota; however, the law that created the quota contains relatively weak sanctions for parties that do not abide by it (Miguel 2008).

National quotas, by helping to overcome women's underrepresentation, can certainly impact the public policy process, prodding it to provide more policies supportive of women's interests. Yet, research does suggest that quotas at the national level can have negative impacts, as well. In their study of Argentina, Franceschet and Piscopo (2008, p. 393) argue that "quota laws complicate both aspects of substantive representation. Quotas generate mandates for female legislators to represent women's interests, while also reinforcing negative stereotypes about women's capacities as politicians." Quotas, therefore, may increase women's representation but may also undermine the reputation of female legislators who obtain their seats through quotas. That such women won their position through a process different from that followed by male legislators suggests to some observers that they obtained their seats more easily and, perhaps, in an undemocratic fashion.

Supporters of national quotas often cite the need to increase women's representation in order to stimulate women's political activity. Since national quotas can increase the level of women's legislative representation, they may spur greater activity among women more broadly as political aspirants observe female legislators active on the national stage. Zetterberg (2009, p. 717), however, casts doubt on this phenomenon by showing, in a study of Latin American countries, that the presence of quota legislation "appears to not be positively associated with women's political engagement." Thus, the use of quotas may not spur women to more political activity.

The Logic of National Quota Adoption

When do political actors push to adopt national quotas? Several factors may explain why actors move to enact either compulsory party quotas or reserved-seat quotas. Parties have often been seen as the primary obstacle to women's legislative representation (Frechette, Maniquet, and Morelli 2008; Lovenduski and Norris 1993). In fact, Bonomi, Brosio, and Tommaso (2006) argue that quotas are unlikely to occur in systems where parties themselves are the main cause of women's underrepresentation. Yet, in chapter 5, we showed that parties can overcome these obstacles to adopt voluntary party quotas. The logic behind parties' decisions to support national quotas shows a striking similarity to the logic that underpins parties' decisions to adopt voluntary party quotas.

Parties may opt to support or oppose national quotas for strategic reasons. Party actors may be uncertain about electoral outcomes, creating openings for those who support quotas to cast them as a tool to increase party vote (Baldez 2004). Thus, the need to compete may push parties to support national quotas as a way to woo voters. In fact, Krook (2005) notes that, in India, parties voiced support for national quotas publicly to curry favor with certain voters while at the same time doing little to implement them. Some parties may find it impossible to adopt a national quota if the quota does not fit well within preexisting patterns of party competition, as was the case in India (Randall 2006).

Resistance to quotas within the party can be overcome, however. In particular, the opposition may fold as the result of strong lobbying by female activists. There is evidence that national quotas have been adopted after successful organizing and lobbying by female activists in a number of countries (Bruhn 2003; Carrio 2005; Craske 1999; Powley 2005; Siregar 2006). In some cases, cross-party coalitions of female activists pushed for the adoption of quotas (Carrio 2005). Just as in the case of voluntary party quotas, the level of women's political activity strongly impacts the adoption of national quotas.

The level of opposition to national quotas within a political party may also depend on the party's ideology. Left-wing parties are often more supportive of national quotas, just as they are often more supportive of voluntary party quotas (Bruhn 2003). In France, while the feminist movement concentrated on other issues, women within the Socialist Party pushed the idea of quotas back in the 1970s (Krook 2005).

Opposition to national quotas may also depend upon the electoral system. For male incumbents in a closed-list proportional-representation system, a compulsory quota represents a direct threat, given that parties will need to meet the quota by prioritizing female candidates at the expense of male candidates (Frechette, Maniquet, and Morelli 2008). Any type of candidate quota can threaten the reelection of male candidates; therefore, one would expect them to oppose such quotas. Yet, Frechette, Maniquet, and Morelli (2008) argue that male candidates' fear of quotas is lower in single-member district-majority systems. Using the adoption of the 2000 Parity Law in France, they show that male incumbents benefited from the law because of an electoral bias that favors men. Male incumbents are, therefore, more likely to support a quota if they operate in electoral systems that do not allow women to obtain the full benefit of the quota because of electoral bias.[2]

In the previous chapter, we found that parties often adopt voluntary party quotas in response to the decisions by other parties to adopt them. Research on national quotas finds a similar process. Countries are more likely to adopt national quotas when they see other countries within their region doing so (Gray 2003; Powley 2005). Relationships between political activists in different countries often speed this policy diffusion process (Bruhn 2003). Powley (2005) points out that activists in the Rwandan Patriotic Front were exposed to gender-equity policies in Uganda and knew of the important role played by women in the African National Congress in South Africa. As other countries in the region adopt quotas, a political leader may fear being considered backward if he does not improve women's representation (Tripp and Kang 2008). Thus, the adoption of a national quota can be impacted by regional policy diffusion.

The existence of regional patterns in national quota adoption points to another critical factor that may explain quota adoption—international norms. Existing research argues that the existence of international commitments to gender equality can influence the adoption of national quotas (Krook 2006a, 2006b, 2007a, 2009). The 1995 Platform of Action drafted by the UN Beijing Conference is the best example of this international commitment. The platform was greeted favorably by many political actors and governments (Tripp and Kang 2008). Thus, countries may adopt national quotas in order to live up to international expectations.

As one country in a region adopts such measures, others may follow, not because they agree with the normative commitment to gender equality but because they fear that not to adopt quotas while their neighbors do so would make them seem backward (Tripp and Kang 2008). In fact, feminist activists in the Nordic countries often pointed to the better records of other governments to push their own countries toward greater equality (Freidnevall,

Dahlerup, and Skjeie 2006). This competition to appear modern may compel countries to adopt quotas to avoid the appearance of falling behind regional neighbors.

Contagion's Influence on National Quotas

The influence of a female executive or the presence of a substantial number of women in the legislature may be particularly important to the adoption of national quotas. Because these quotas, unlike voluntary quotas, are codified in law, they require a substantial number of political actors committed to increasing women's representation. This commitment may be more likely where women have made some headway in gaining political office.

The adoption of national quotas may also be spurred by the adoption of voluntary party quotas. In Belgium, a compulsory party quota was adopted only after the adoption of voluntary party quotas by several parties (Meier 2004). As the number of parties with quotas increases, the resistance to such measures may dissipate. In fact, the success of these quotas can increase the pressure on other parties to adopt them. It may also impel activists to push for the next step—the adoption of a national quota. Research on the causes of national quotas points to causes that differ from those associated with voluntary party quotas. Activists who seek the adoption of voluntary party quotas often cite the low level of women's representation as a justification for implementing such guidelines. Similarly, activists leverage this issue to spur the adoption of national quotas. Yet, the research on national quotas points out that their adoption often occurs, in part, as the result of broader crises and political concerns. Baldez (2006, pp. 104–105) argues that, "in Latin American countries, support for gender quotas (as well as quotas for youth and sometimes for indigenous peoples) is closely linked to high levels of distrust in the political system."

Reform and democracy in Latin America allowed this distrust to become institutionalized in quotas that improve women's legislative representation (Baldez 2004). The deep changes in political institutions ushered in by democratic consolidation can create the necessary space for the endorsement of national-level quotas as a legitimate option to address systemic discrimination.

We can see a similar process at work in Rwanda. In the aftermath of the Rwandan genocide, the new constitution mandated that 30 percent of legislative seats were reserved for women. Feminists groups as well as nongovernmental organizations (NGOs) organized to push for the inclusion of a reserved-seat quota (Powley 2005). Yet, the support of the government and of the Rwandan Patriotic Front (RPF) was essential for the inclusion of the quota provision, as well. Powley (2005) noted that the discrimination against the RPF and the Tutsi minority that backed the party made them more supportive of a reserved-seat quota as a legitimate method to address discrimination against women.

National quotas represent a more drastic, less gradual solution to gender inequality than voluntary party quotas. Baldez (2006, p. 103) states that "[t]heir appeal derives in part from the failure of more gradual efforts to change the masculine culture of politics." These more gradual efforts are most often associated with the experience of the Nordic countries, where factors such as the use of favorable electoral systems and the early implementation of voluntary party quotas led to impressive increases in women's representation. Dahlerup (2005) argues that many new democracies that have had histories of excluding women from politics are opting for a fast-track approach that involves the use of national quotas. This explains why we see reserved-seat quotas being adopted in places like Rwanda, Uganda, Niger, and Morocco but have no examples of reserved-seat quotas in Western Europe. In fact, advocates of national quotas may face fewer obstacles in new democracies. Dahlerup (2005, p. 148) notes that "history seems to prove that the implementation of a quota system is made easier in a new political system than in an older one, where most seats might be occupied, and consequently a conflict may arise between the interests of new groups and those of the incumbents."

The Distribution of National Quotas

Using our dataset of democracies between 1945 and 2006, we can examine the patterns of national quota adoption. We present separate patterns for compulsory party quotas and reserved-seat quotas. In our data, we have information concerning twenty-one compulsory party quotas and seven reserved-seat quotas.

Figures 6.1 and 6.2 present the distribution of compulsory party quotas and reserved-seat quotas by year from our sample. Both figures clearly show that national quotas are a recent phenomenon. Our first compulsory party quota appears in 1991; our first reserved-seat quota appears in 1989. The figures also demonstrate that compulsory party quotas are more common than reserved-seat quotas.

When we examine the regional distribution of national quotas, we also see a distinctive pattern. Figure 6.3 presents the percentage of compulsory party quotas by region between 1989 and 2006. The first compulsory quotas

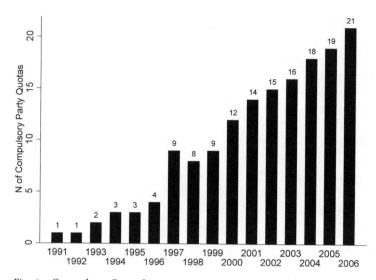

Fig. 6.1. Compulsory Party Quotas, 1991–2006

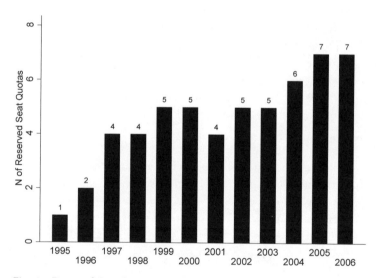

Fig. 6.2. Reserved-Seat Quotas, 1989–2006

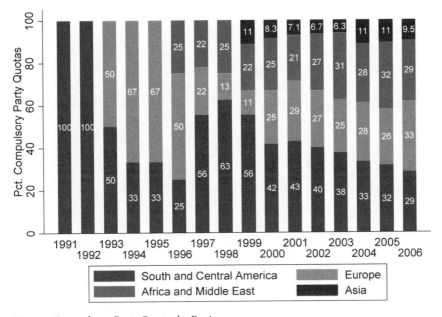

Fig. 6.3. Compulsory Party Quotas by Region

were adopted in South and Central America; they spread to Europe in the early 1990s. By 2006, the majority of nations (58 percent) with compulsory quotas were located in either Europe or Latin America. Compulsory quotas spread to Africa and the Middle East in the mid-1990s; by 2006, 33 percent of compulsory quotas were located in these regions. Compulsory quotas did not appear in Asia until 1999. Conspicuous by their absence from the list of countries with compulsory party quotas are North American countries. The regional distribution of compulsory quotas gives credence to the fast-track argument, given that these quotas appeared in regions such as Africa and Latin America during periods in which democratic transitions took place. Yet, we also see evidence that compulsory party quotas exist in Europe in older, established democracies.

Figure 6.4 presents our sample's regional distribution of reserved-seat quotas between 1989 and 2006. The regional distribution of reserved-seat quotas appears to reflect the fast-track explanation. All of the quotas in our sample are to be found outside Europe and North America. The first reserved-seat quotas were adopted in Asia; they later spread to South and Central America and Africa in the mid-1990s. By 2006, fully 43 percent of reserved-seat quotas were located in Asian countries.

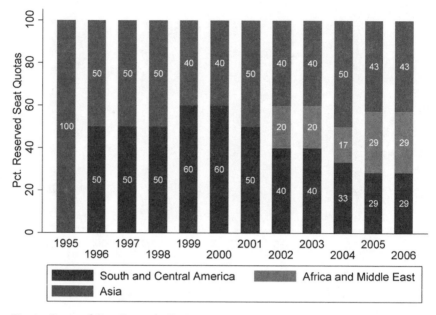

Fig. 6.4. Reserved-Seat Quotas by Region

Modeling National Quota Adoption

What factors explain the adoption of national quotas? Do we have evidence that contagion matters? To help answer these questions, we use our dataset of democratic countries between 1945 and 2006. Using this dataset, we model the onset and the incidence of both compulsory seat quotas and reserved-seat quotas. Thus, we avoid the assumption that the factors that lead to the onset of one type of quota are the same as those that lead to the onset of the other.

The Onset of National Quotas

To model onset for both types of national quotas, we employ Cox proportional-hazards models. Thus, we model the time to the adoption of both quotas. We tested each of our models to ensure that they meet the proportional-hazards assumption. For independent variables that do not meet this assumption, we include an interaction term between the problematic variable and time (Box-Steffensmeier and Jones 2003). It is possible that the errors in our model will be correlated by country (i.e., across panels). To deal with the potential of heteroscedasticity, we calculate robust standard errors clustered on individual countries. We employ the Breslow method to deal with ties.

We measure the effects of contagion with several variables. First, we include the percentage of women in the legislature (Inter-Parliamentary Union 2008a). We also include a variable indicating the presence of a female chief executive (Gleditsch and Chiozza 2009; Worldwide Guide to Women in Leadership 2009). If the presence of women in other democratic institutions influences the adoption of national quotas, then these variables should be positively correlated with the onset of national quotas.

Contagion may operate through the existence of quotas, as well. In our model for compulsory party quotas, we include the number of parties with voluntary party quotas. There is evidence that, in some countries, the existence of voluntary quotas spurs the adoption of compulsory party quotas.

For both the compulsory party quota model and the reserved-seat quota models, we need to control for regional policy diffusion. Existing research suggests that countries may adopt quotas in response to their adoption in other countries. Consequently, we include variables that measure the number of countries in the region with each type of quota. These variables should control for regional quota dissemination.

We control for socioeconomic factors by including both GDP per capita in constant U.S dollars and the rate of female labor force participation (OECD 2009; World Bank 2009). Countries with longer histories of universal suffrage may be more likely to adopt national quotas; therefore, we include years since universal suffrage as a control variable (Inter-Parliamentary Union 2008b). To control for electoral system effects, we include the natural log of district magnitude (Beck et al. 2001; Golder 2005; Johnson and Wallack 2008).

The research on national quotas argues that states may prefer to fast-track women's representation. In addition, states that have recently transitioned to democracy may also be more likely to adopt them. To control for these processes, we include a variable that measures the number of years since a country's most recent democratic transition. A transition occurs when a country is democratic at time t but was nondemocratic at $t-1$.[3]

We include several regional dummy variables, as well. Unfortunately, several of the regional variables we used in previous models proved to be collinear in our national quota onset models, so we were forced to drop some of these variables from the model. Thus, we can account for some but not all the regional variation that may influence adoption.

Table 6.1 presents the results of Cox proportional-hazards models of the onset of compulsory party quotas (Model 1) and reserved-seat quotas (Model

Table 6.1. Onset of Compulsory Party Quotas and Reserved Seat Quotas

Variable	Model 1 Compulsory Coeff.	Std. Errors	Model 2 Reserved Seats Coeff.	Std. Errors
Log of GDP per Capita Constant U.S. $	1.122	0.342	0.630	0.301
Female Labor Force Participation	0.952**	0.018	1.117*	0.073
Years since Suffrage	0.992	0.013	0.996	0.020
Years Democratic	0.911**	0.035	1.010	0.018
Log of District Magnitude	1.087	0.152	0.540**	0.130
Percent Women in Legislature	0.941*	0.032	0.928	0.070
Female Executive in Year	0.617	0.712	16.357	29.532
N Party Quotas	1.433	0.344		
N Regional Compulsory Party Quotas	1.973***	0.224		
N Reserved Seat Quotas			6.128***	3.855
South and Central America	0.528	0.387	46.277*	102.955
Africa and Middle East	0.887	0.765	0.625	0.877
Asia	0.657	0.635		
Years Democratic * Log of Time	1.002**	0.001	1.002**	0.001
Observations	2053		2148	
Countries	109		109	
X^2	86.28***		52.94***	

* p < 0.10, ** p < 0.05, *** p < 0.01

2). If we examine Model 1, we find several interesting results. There is no cor-relation between wealth and the onset of a compulsory party quota. Thus, the traditional relationship between wealth and women's representation that we found in other areas is not present here. We also find no evidence that quota onset is related to the number of years since democratic suffrage.

The literature on national quotas suggests that they are more likely to be adopted by countries seeking to fast-track gender equity. This approach is often associated with new democracies. We find evidence to support this contention in our model of the onset of compulsory party quotas. An in-crease of one standard deviation in the years democratic variable decreases the hazard of compulsory party quota adoption by 97 percent. This finding, coupled with the absence of an independent effect on quota adoption of wealth and years since suffrage, supports the notion that the onset of a com-pulsory party quota is less likely to occur in more established democracies.

We find no evidence that the type of electoral system has an impact on the onset of compulsory party quotas. The results indicate that the hazard of quota adoption increases as district magnitude does; however, the variable is not statistically significant.

In terms of contagion, we find interesting and somewhat contradictory results. On the one hand, increasing the number of women in the legislature and the presence of a female executive appear to delay the adoption of compulsory party quotas. Increasing the percentage of women in the legislature by one standard deviation decreases the hazard by just over 40 percent. The presence of a female executive decreases the hazard of compulsory quota adoption by just over 96 percent. Thus, we find little evidence that the presence of women in the executive or the legislature hastens the onset of compulsory party quota adoption. However, this result does lend support to the fast-track argument. The results here suggest that the absence of women's representation spurs quota adoption. This makes sense, given the logic of the fast-track argument that views quota adoption as a response to weak levels of women's representation.

We find no evidence that the presence of parties with voluntary quotas affects the onset of compulsory party quotas. The hazard ratio for the number of parties with quotas variable is greater than one, indicating that, as the number of parties with quotas increases, the hazard for compulsory party quotas also increases; however, the variable is not statistically significant. Consequently, we find that the number of parties with voluntary quotas has no independent effect on the onset of a compulsory quota.

Yet, there is strong evidence that regional policy diffusion exists. According to the results of Model 1, a one-country increase in the number of regional countries with a compulsory quota increases the hazard of adoption by 97.3 percent. Countries in regions where other countries have previously adopted a compulsory party quota will, according to our results, adopt such quotas themselves more quickly than countries in regions where few or no countries have adopted compulsory party quotas.

Model 2 in Table 6.1 presents our Cox regression results for reserved-seat quotas. The results demonstrate both similarities and differences between the onset of compulsory party and reserved-seat quotas. We find no evidence that wealth impacts the onset of a reserved-seat quota, similar to what we found in our analysis of voluntary party quotas.

Yet, we do find evidence that women's political mobilization matters. In Model 2, a one standard deviation increase in female labor force participation increases the hazard of quota adoption by more than 340 percent. Thus, while higher rates of female participation reduce the hazard of compulsory party quota onset, they actually increase the hazard of reserved-seat quota adoption. This may reflect differences in the level of women's political mobilization necessary to win adoption of the different types of quotas. Compulsory party quotas may be adopted in countries with weak women's representation as a response to demands by elites or activists for greater equality. A reserved-seat quota represents a stronger, more direct commitment to equality than does a compulsory party quota, since reserved-seat quotas require legislative seats not just the opportunity to compete for seats. Consequently, adoption of such quotas may require greater levels of women's activism.

Neither the years since universal suffrage variable nor the years democratic variable is statistically significant. Thus, we find no evidence that a longer commitment to women's suffrage predisposes a country to the early onset of a reserved-seat quota. In addition, countries with longer democratic histories are neither more nor less likely to adopt a reserved-seat quota.

We find that other socioeconomic and political factors such as wealth, years since suffrage, and democratic persistence have no impact on the adoption of quotas. The fact that time to quota adoption does not depend on these factors means that those countries with longer democratic histories, longer records of suffrage, or greater female political participation do not adopt quotas earlier than other countries. This supports the fast-track contention that countries with quotas are often those with weak levels of women's representation.

Electoral systems do matter; however, they do so in an unexpected way. We find that the onset of a reserved-seat quota is sped up by the existence not of a more proportional electoral system but of a less proportional electoral system. An increase of one standard deviation in the natural log of district magnitude decreases the hazard of adopting a reserved-seat quota by 57 percent. This finding could result from the fact that reserved-seat quotas are a response to women's underrepresentation, which is more likely to be found in less proportional than in more proportional systems.

We do not find evidence of contagion. Both the percentage women in the legislature and the female executive variables are statistically insignificant for the time to adoption of a reserved-seat quota. However, our statistical results provide further evidence of regional policy diffusion. A one-country increase in the number of regional neighbors with a reserved-seat quota increases the hazard of quota adoption by more than 80 percent. This finding supports the view that demonstration effects or competitive pressures push nations toward reserved-seat quotas when neighbors adopt similar quotas.

The Incidence of National Quotas

To model the incidence of national quotas, we create two variables, one indicating the existence of a compulsory party quota in the country in the year and the other indicating the existence of a reserved-seat quota in the country in the year. To model incidence, we use a multilevel mixed-effects logistic

Table 6.2. The Incidence of National Quotas

Variables	Model 3		Model 4	
	Compulsory Party Quota Coeff.	Std. Errors	Reserved Seats Coeff.	Std. Errors
Log of GDP per Capita Constant U.S. $	0.044	0.117	−1.303***	0.328
Female Labor Force Participation	−0.035***	0.009	0.045**	0.021
Years since Suffrage	−0.002	0.006	0.037***	0.014
Years Democratic	0.004	0.004	−0.034*	0.018
Log of District Magnitude	0.286***	0.084	−0.567***	0.193
Percent Women in Legislature$_{t-1}$	−0.033**	0.015	−0.006	0.035
Female Executive in Year$_{t-1}$	−1.060**	0.538	1.179**	0.568
N Party Quotas$_{t-1}$	0.365***	0.095		
N Regional Compulsory Party Quotas	0.419***	0.087		
N Reserved Seat Quotas$_{t-1}$			0.857***	0.241
Constant	−19.615	1001.517	−15.506	1545.260
Region (Variance)	0.131	0.134	3.190	3.141
Observations	2168		2168	
Countries	109		109	
Wald X²	102.42***		47.91***	
L.R. X²	5.19**		18.07***	

* p < 0.10, ** p < 0.05, *** p < 0.01

regression model. This approach allows us to include both fixed and random effects. Since the countries are nested in regions, we use a model with a random intercept for different regions. The remaining variables are calculated using fixed effects.[4]

Model 3 presents the results of our mixed-effects model using the compulsory party quota dependent variable. Wealth is not correlated with compulsory quota incidence; wealthier countries are not more likely to adopt these quotas. We also find that the years since suffrage and years democratic variables are statistically insignificant. Consequently, neither an early adoption of universal suffrage nor a long history of democracy independently impacts the likelihood of a compulsory party quota.

Female labor force matters, however, in an unexpected fashion. The percentage female labor force participation variable is statistically significant but negatively correlated with compulsory party quota adoption. A 1 percent increase in female labor force participation decreases the odds of quota adoption by 3.4 percent. Thus, compulsory party quotas are more likely to be found in those countries with weaker levels of female labor force participation.

We do find evidence of electoral system effects. The natural log of district magnitude variable is statistically significant and positively correlated with the probability of compulsory quota incidence. A one-unit increase in the log of district magnitude increases the odds of quota incidence by 33 percent.

We find that both women's representation in the legislature and the female executive variables are statistically significant but negatively correlated with the incidence of compulsory party quotas. A 1 percent increase in women's legislative representation decreases the odds of compulsory party quota adoption by 3.3 percent. Having a female chief executive decreases the odds of compulsory party quota incidence by 65.4 percent. Thus, we find that contagion in terms of the presence of women in the legislature and the executive branch discourages the adoption of compulsory list quotas.

We do, however, find strong effects based on the number of quota parties and the regional diffusion of compulsory party quotas. Increasing the number of quota parties by one party increases the odds of compulsory party quota incidence by 44 percent. Increasing by one the number of neighboring countries with a quota increases the probability of compulsory party quota incidence by 52 percent.

As expected, we find significant differences among regions based upon our random intercepts in Model 3. Table 6.3 presents values for the random intercepts.[5] The values of the random intercepts demonstrate that compulsory party quotas are more likely to be adopted in South and Central America, in Africa, and in the Middle East. Countries in other regions are less likely to use such quotas.

Model 4 in Table 6.2 presents the results of our model of reserved-seat quota incidence. The results are interesting and demonstrate that the factors that account for compulsory party quotas are, on the whole, different from those that explain reserved-seat quotas. The GDP per capita variable is statistically significant and negatively correlated with the incidence of a reserved-seat quota. Thus, wealthier countries are less likely to adopt reserved-seat quotas. This finding is consistent with the fast-track literature. A one-unit increase in the GDP per capita variable decreases the odds of reserved-seat quota incidence by 72.8 percent.

Table 6.3. Values of Regional Random Effects, Model 3

Region	Random Effect
South and Central America	0.484
North America	−0.068
Europe	−0.386
Africa and Middle East	0.074
Asia	−0.070

Countries that adopt reserved-seat quotas, on average, have both a longer history of suffrage and higher levels of women's labor force participation. In our analysis, both the years since suffrage variable and the female labor force participation variable are statistically significant and positively correlated with the incidence of a reserved-seat quota. A 1 percent increase in female labor force participation increases the odds of quota adoption by 4.6 percent. A one-year increase in years since universal suffrage increases the odds of quota adoption by 3.7 percent.

We find further support for the fast-track argument as an explanation for quota adoption in the results of the years democratic variable. The variable is statistically significant and negatively correlated with reserved-seat quota incidence. A one-year increase in the number of years democratic reduces the odds of reserved-seat quota incidence by 3.4 percent. Thus, more established democracies are less likely to adopt reserved-seat quotas.

In Model 4, district magnitude is statistically significant and negatively correlated with the likelihood of a reserved-seat quota—the opposite of what we found for compulsory quotas. A one-unit increase in the log of district magnitude decreases the odds of a reserved-seat quota incidence by 43.2 percent. Again, this result is consistent with the idea that reserved-seat quotas are adopted in countries where there are obstacles to women's representation and where groups are interested in finding a quick solution to the problem of women's legislative representation. Thus, the incidence of a reserved-seat quota is not consistent with traditional electoral system arguments.

Do we have evidence of contagion in our analysis of the incidence of reserved-seat quotas? The results of Model 4 do in fact demonstrate just this. On the one hand, the level of women's representation has no independent impact on quota incidence. The percentage of women in the legislature variable is negatively correlated; however, it is statistically insignificant. Thus, the existing level of women's representation in the legislature did not impact quota incidence independent of other factors.

On the other hand, we see strong evidence in the presence of a female executive. The female executive dummy variable is statistically significant and positively correlated with the incidence of quotas. Having a female chief executive increases the incidence of reserved-seat quotas by 225 percent. Thus, the election of a female chief executive positively impacts the likelihood of a reserved-seat quota.

We also find strong evidence of regional policy diffusion. The number of countries in the region with a reserved-seat quota is both statistically significant and positively correlated with quota adoption. A one-country increase in this variable increases the odds of quota incidence by 135 percent.

Table 6.4. Values of Regional Random Effects, Model 4

Region	Random Effect
South and Central America	2.639
North America	−0.001
Europe	−1.073
Africa and Middle East	−1.320
Asia	0.206

As we found in Model 3, Model 4 reveals significant differences among regions. Table 6.4 presents values for the random intercepts. We find that countries in Asia and in South and Central America are more likely to adopt reserved-seat quotas.

Discussion of Results

The empirical analysis presented here points to several interesting conclusions about the nature of national quota adoption and incidence. First, it is clear that the processes that drive compulsory party quota adoption are different from those that drive reserved-seat quota adoption. Wealth appears to play no role in the onset or incidence of a compulsory party quota; however, it is clear that poorer countries are more likely than wealthy ones to have reserved-seat quotas. We find differences in terms of the effect of electoral institutions. While countries with more proportional systems are more likely to have a compulsory party quota, they are less likely to feature reserved-seat quotas. We also find differences in terms of the effect of two main elements of contagion—the percentage of women in the legislature and the presence of a female executive. While the percentage of women in the legislature negatively affects both the onset and the incidence of a compulsory party quota, it appears to have no independent impact on the incidence or onset of a reserved-seat quota. In addition, the presence of a female executive has a conflicting impact on the incidence of national quotas: while the presence of a female executive reduces the probability of the incidence of a compulsory party quota, it increases the probability of the incidence of a reserved-seat quota.

Second, the results do support the logic behind the fast-track argument. The fact that wealthy countries with long histories of democracy are not more likely to implement a national quota indicates that such quotas will not typically be found in more established democracies. In addition, the fact that women's legislative representation is not positively correlated with the adoption of national quotas strongly supports the fast-track argument, which contends that countries adopt such quotas to speed up the process of women's inclusion. The fact that women's labor force participation is negatively correlated with the incidence of a compulsory party quota further supports this point of view.

Yet, the results for reserved-seat quotas do suggest something a bit different. A higher level of women's labor force participation increases the hazard of quota adoption, as well as the probability of quota incidence. Moreover, the incidence of reserved-seat quota adoption is more likely in countries with a female executive and a longer history of women's universal suffrage. Does this suggest that the fast-track logic is incorrect? We argue that the logic is not so much wrong but that it may need more development. The adoption of a reserved-seat quota represents a powerful commitment to women's legislative equality. Thus, it may represent a desire to increase women's representation quickly in the face of significant obstacles; however, it may be possible only in countries with a commitment to women's equality in other areas, as indicated by the longer term of suffrage or an elected female chief executive.

Finally, we have strong evidence that regional policy diffusion matters for both types of quotas. Countries located in regions with greater numbers of national quotas have a higher probability of adopting such quotas than other countries and have a higher probability of adopting a quota system. Thus, we see strong evidence that the adoption of national quotas is sped by regional, competitive pressures. We further examine the effects of these variables in the critical case of Ireland.

Gender Quotas in Ireland

In March 2009, the Irish Labour Party proposed a Gender Parity Bill to establish a compulsory party quota for elections to the Dáil. Parties would lose half of their public funding if they failed to grant women at least 20 percent of their electoral nominations. This threshold would increase to 33 percent in seven years, then 40 percent in another seven years. The bill contained a sunset provision that would remove the quota after twenty-one years. The bill, however, was not adopted. The issue of a gender quota was again raised by Fine Gael leader Enda Kenny one year later, in March 2010, but the idea was rejected by the Fine Gael parliamentary party. The focus on quotas was not new in Ireland. The National Women's Council of Ireland had recommended a quota previously in 1992, and the Democracy Commission, an independent commission that examined the state of democracy in Ireland, advocated one in 2005. The National Women's Council of Ireland suggested a 40 percent quota in 2002. The chair of the council, Grainne Healy, argued that, at

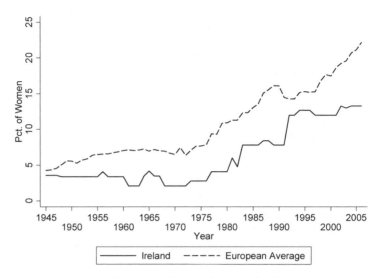

Fig. 6.5. Percentage of Women in the Legislature, Ireland versus Europe

the current pace of improvement, "we will have equal Dáil representation by 2036" (O'Doherty 2002, p. 5).

That political leaders and activists have suggested a compulsory party quota should not come as a surprise, given that the percentage of women in the Irish Dáil is significantly lower than their representation in the governing bodies of other European democracies. Figure 6.5 plots the percentage of women in the lower house of the Irish legislature and the average percentage of women in European legislatures between 1945 and 2006. The figure clearly demonstrates that Ireland remains significantly below the average European country in terms of women's legislative representation.

What explains Ireland's poor showing? Some scholars point to Ireland's political culture. On the basis of a survey of female Irish legislators, Knight et al. (2004, p. 16) contend that, since there is significant agreement among respondents that child care is an important obstacle to women's legislative careers, "traditional cultural attitudes" that prevent women's equality remain active. For some researchers, traditional values that reinforce women's conventional gender roles reflect, in part, strong Catholic traditions in Ireland (Galligan 2005; Galligan and Wilford 1999; Randall and Smyth 1987). Thus, the below-average level of women's legislative representation in Ireland is in part a result of cultural traditions that create obstacles for women's equality.

The notion that Irish cultural traditions undermine women's legislative representation is not universally shared. McElroy and Marsh (2009, 2011) analyze candidate-level voting results, candidate survey data, and voter surveys and find no sign of gender discrimination among voters. Their results suggest that voters are just as likely to vote for female candidates as they are to vote for male candidates. In addition, voters are not predisposed against supporting female legislative candidates. Thus, they conclude that, "[i]f there are too few women in Dáil Éireann, it is not down to the voters" (McElroy and Marsh 2011, p. 13).

The Irish electoral system may also explain the country's poor record on women's legislative representation. Ireland employs a single-transferable vote (STV) system in multimember constituencies. In this system, voters are asked to rank individual candidates. Often, voters must rank candidates from the same party. Thus, STV creates significant incentives for candidates to cultivate personal votes, and research shows that, while party is not unimportant, voters often cast ballots according to their views of individual candidates (McElroy and Marsh 2009). As discussed previously, systems with strong personal vote incentives have been found to undermine women's representation in other contexts (Thames and Williams 2010). Yet, Ireland's system does elect between three and five members per district; thus, it should be more proportional than, for example, a single-member district system. Current research seems split on the extent to which the STV system undermines women's representation. Only three countries use STV at the national level—Ireland, Malta, and Australia. Two of these nations have a consistently poor record of women's representation, while Australia is well above average (Hirczy 1995). Schwindt-Bayer, Malecki, and Crisp (2010) argue that STV has no generalizable effect on women's representation given the differences between Ireland, Malta, and Australia. Their research finds that Irish female candidates face significant discrimination based, they argue, upon Ireland's traditional political culture.

Other factors besides the electoral system may be at work. McElroy and Marsh (2009) point to supply-side factors. Potentially, differences in the level of ambitions of male and female candidates may explain why so few Irish women get elected to the Dáil. In addition, the fact that female candidates do not perform better than male candidates may give party leaders less incentive to nominate women (McElroy and Marsh 2009). Parties, especially larger ones that tend to feature lower turnover among candidates, may also simply not encourage female candidates (McElroy and Marsh 2011). Thus, parties and their leaders, not voters, may be the true obstacle to women's representation.

Given what we know about compulsory party quota adoption, should we expect Ireland to adopt one? Table 6.5 compares the averages of Ireland and

Table 6.5. Comparing Ireland to Europe

Variable	Ireland Avg.	European Avg.	Difference	P Value
Log of District Magnitude	1.4	2.2	0.794	0.000
Female Labor Force Participation	41.9	56.9	15.0	0.000
N Quota Parties	0.749	0.758	0.75	0.479
Percent Women in the Legislature	6.2	13.2	7.0	0.000

Note: P values from a difference of means t-test.

Europe for several of the variables from our dataset. If we simply average the percentage of women in the legislature across all years in our dataset for Ireland and Europe, we see a stark difference. Women's representation in Europe was twice that in Ireland. Two factors we found in chapter 2 that were correlated with women's representation—log of district magnitude and female labor force participation—are, on average, substantially lower among our Irish observations in than in our European observations. Ireland had only slightly fewer parties with gender quotas on average than did the other European countries.

Yet, Table 6.5 also suggests that it is not entirely out of the realm of what is to be expected that Ireland might adopt compulsory party quotas on the basis of the models we presented earlier. We did find that compulsory party quotas were more likely to be adopted in systems with greater district magnitudes. However, we also found that countries with lower percentages both of female labor force participation and of women in the legislature were more likely to adopt compulsory party quotas. Thus, we have some reason to believe that a compulsory party quota would be more likely in Ireland than in other European countries.

To assess further the potential for compulsory party quota adoption, we calculate predicted probabilities of compulsory quota incidence using the results from Model 3 in Table 6.2. First, we calculate the observed predicted probability for each year where we set all variables at the observed levels of Ireland in the year. Then, we calculate a simulated predicted probability where we set the log of the district magnitude variable at the European average in the year, with the rest of the variables set at the observed levels of Ireland in a year. Thus, we are simulating the effect of electoral reform on the probability of compulsory party quota incidence. Finally, for both probabilities, we plot the 95 percent confidence intervals around the predictions.

Figure 6.6 plots the observed and simulated predicted probabilities of compulsory quota incidence in Ireland from 1991 through 2006. The observed predicted probability that reflects the estimates from our model using the Irish values suggests an increasing probability of compulsory party quota incidence. Given the fact that such plans have already been actively pursued in the Dáil, the increasing probability should not surprise us. We plot the simulated impact of increasing the log of district magnitude to European levels, as well. As we would expect, increasing the district magnitude does increase the predicted probability for every year. However, the impact is relatively modest and not statistically different from our observed prediction.

What about contagion and regional policy diffusion? The results from our model of compulsory party quota incidence indicate that quota adoption was positively correlated with both the number of quota parties and the number of countries in the region with compulsory quotas. We simulated the impact of increasing levels of both the number of party quotas and the number of regional quotas on compulsory party quota incidence in Ireland. To do this, we first estimated the predicted probability, as we did previously, using observed levels of the variables based on the Irish case. Then, we estimated a simulated probability by doubling the number of quota parties in Ireland for every year. The Labour Party and the Workers Party adopted party quotas in 1991; the Green Party adopted a party quota in 1992.

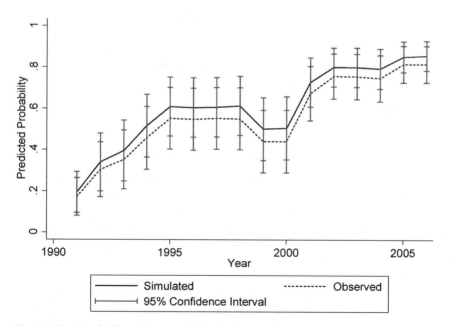

Fig. 6.6. Simulated Effect of Increased District Magnitude

Figure 6.7 graphs the observed predicted probability and the simulated predicted probability, which we calculated by doubling the number of quota parties. The simulated predicted probability is significantly greater than that of the observed probability for most of the years for which we calculated probabilities, in particular after 1992. Yet, the differences are not statistically different from the observed values at the 95 percent level. If we calculate 90 percent confidence intervals, the results are statistically significant.[6] Thus, there is some evidence, based on our simulation, that contagion through party adoption of voluntary quotas could increase the probability of the incidence of a compulsory party quota in Ireland.

We can explore the impact of regional policy diffusion by simulating the impact of an increase in the number of countries with a compulsory party quota on the incidence of quota adoption in Ireland. We do this by increasing the number of European countries with a compulsory party quota by 20 percent. Figure 6.8 plots the observed predicted probabilities and the simulated ones created by increasing the number of countries in Europe with a compulsory party quota by 20 percent. Not only are the simulated probabilities substantially higher than the observed probabilities, but also the difference between them is statistically significant at the 95 percent level. Thus, if more countries in Europe adopted quotas, we would expect the probability of compulsory party quota incidence in Ireland to increase dramatically. The impact of policy diffusion in terms of the regional spread of national quotas would, according to our empirical model and simulations, increase the chances that Ireland would follow with a national quota.

Conclusion

National gender quotas, whether compulsory party quotas or reserved-seat quotas, are rare. Very few countries make the type of commitment to legislative gender equity that is embodied in a quota that mandates that women have a predetermined percentage of nominations in an election or seats in a legislature. In this chapter, we undertook a statistical analysis of the onset and the incidence of both types of national quotas. The results provide us with critical insights on why some countries utilize quotas and others do not. Our main insight is that compulsory party quotas and reserved-seat quotas are two different animals. The factors that explain one do not necessarily explain the other. They differ in terms of the impact of wealth, labor force participation, years since suffrage, district magnitude, the percentage of women in the legislature, and the impact of a female chief executive. Thus, when we

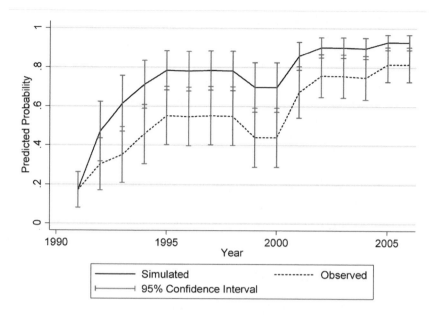

Fig. 6.7. Simulated Effect of Increased Number of Quota Parties

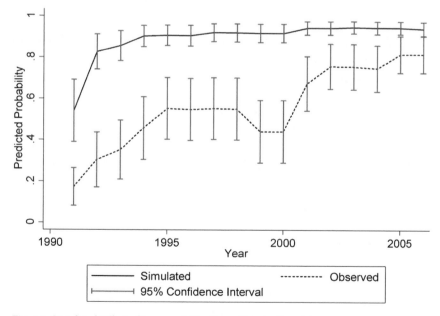

Fig. 6.8. Simulated Effect of Increased Number of Quota Countries

analyze national quotas, we need to keep in mind the important differences between them.

We do find evidence that national quotas represent an alternative, fast-track approach to gender equity. The fact that national quotas are not often found in wealthy, advanced democracies is an indication of this. In addition, the fact that women's legislative representation has a null or negative impact on quotas further supports the argument that national quotas are more likely to be adopted in countries that want to address quickly gender imbalances.

Perhaps the strongest predictor of national quota onset and incidence is regional diffusion. We find strong evidence that the number of national quotas of either type in a region predicts both the incidence and onset of quotas in individual countries within that region. This finding is clearly highlighted in our analysis of Ireland, where we found that the probability of quota adoption there increased steadily as the number of countries in Europe with a quota increased.

What about contagion? The evidence for the impact of contagion on national quota adoption is mixed. Women's legislative representation has either no impact or a negative impact on the adoption of quotas. Thus, we find that women's legislative representation may actually hinder the adoption of quotas. We find that the presence of a female executive discourages compulsory party quota adoption but encourages reserved-seat quota adoption. Thus, there is no general impact of executive contagion on national quotas. We did find evidence that the adoption of voluntary party quotas spurred the adoption of compulsory party quotas, suggesting that, once parties adopt such quotas, resistance to a national-level commitment to gender equity dissipates.

7

Conclusion

Why Contagion Matters

This book set out to examine the influences of contagion on women's political representation. As we have defined it here, contagion is the influence of women's participation and political gains in one institution on others. To examine these influences, we studied legislatures, executive offices, high courts, and the adoption of voluntary and compulsory quotas in democracies across the globe from 1945 to 2006. We find strong evidence that one institution can influence others. Our results suggest that future work should consider such influences as we further explore women's political participation.

While there is strong evidence of contagion overall, the results of this book show that contagion's influence manifests itself in different ways, depending on the institution under study. When we considered legislatures, we found that the lagged percentage of women in the legislature was a significant predictor of women's political participation. This suggests that women's political participation is a slow-building process in some democracies, but even small gains in the percentage of women can have significant effects down the road.

Additionally, we found that quotas had a significant influence on women's representation in the legislature. While the results are hardly surprising given the goal of most quota laws, they are nonetheless significant. As the number of parties with voluntary quotas increases, so does women's participation in the legislature. Similarly, compulsory party and reserved-seat quotas substantially influence women's participation. The results point to a potential avenue for increasing women's participation in the United States —adopting a quota law.

In the executive branch of government we see substantially fewer gains for women over the course of our study, but the effects of contagion are significant, nonetheless. In looking at the factors that raise the probability of a female executive, we found that the percentage of women in the legislature and the presence of a reserved-seat quota were both significantly related to a higher probability of a female executive. While female executives remain rare, they do become more likely as women gain traction in other ways. Moreover, countries can decrease the time to electing a female executive by simply enacting a quota law of any type.

The results for the executive model are somewhat more surprising than those for the legislature. While quota laws were meant to increase women's legislative representation, they were not intended to influence women's participation in other avenues of political life. Yet, the results for the executive chapter show that they clearly do. Our discussion of the possible election of a female president in France illustrates how important the combination of other avenues of participation, rather than any individual factor, is for increasing the probability of a female executive. While France already has a substantial gender quota, it is still unlikely to elect a female president until a substantial number of women serve in legislative office.

The influence of contagion on the participation of women in the judiciary shows slightly different results, likely because of the differences in institutions and statistical models. As we found in our 2008 study, women's representation on high courts in OECD countries continues to be influenced by the percentage of women in the legislature. Japan is a clear example of this. Given that legislatures are often involved in the selection of judges, because they either select or approve judicial nominees, diversifying the legislature should lead to a more diverse bench. The connection between having more women in the legislature and the selection of more female judges is clear.

What is more surprising is that contagion fails to influence women's representation on high courts in an expanded sample of countries outside the advanced, industrialized OECD. While a number of other variables had different effects across the two models (discussed later), the results suggest that all high courts may not be comparable, so understanding women's gains in this institution may require more theoretical work about selection and judicial independence.

Because the first gains by women came in the institutions of the legislature and the executive, we considered the influences of contagion in more traditional institutions before examining its influence on other types of institutions, such as parties and quotas. Nonetheless, we still find strong results for the influences of contagion when we move to newer institutions. The adoption of voluntary party quotas, for example, shows contagion's significant effects on the time to adoption and the incidence of voluntary quotas. Increasing the percentage of women in the legislature decreases the time to the adoption of a voluntary party quota and increases the probability any party will adopt a voluntary quota, in part because there are more politically powerful women to push for such initiatives.

Similarly, the presence of compulsory party quota laws and of greater numbers of other parties with quotas significantly reduces the time to adoption of a voluntary quota for any particular party. It also increases the probability that any party will adopt this type of quota. These results suggest that, as parties see the costs of such measures changing, they move toward adoption. The presence of a compulsory quota means that a voluntary party quota comes at no cost—the resulting change in the number of female legislators is already determined, so the party can enjoy the benefit of creating the voluntary quota to curry favor with women. In like fashion, as the parties around them adopt voluntary quotas, the pressure on any individual party to adopt a voluntary quota increases, as well; they need to stay competitive in the electorate. The Swedish case best highlights this phenomenon; were it not for left-wing parties' early adoption of voluntary quotas, Sweden might not have such a significant number of women participating in politics today.

The influence of contagion on the adoption of national quotas (either compulsory party or reserved seat) is more mixed than what we saw for voluntary quotas. Contagion had no effect on the time to adoption of a national quota, and the incidence of quotas could be negatively influenced by women's gains in other offices, which we discuss more fully later. The number of parties with voluntary quotas was positively associated with the adoption of a compulsory party quota, while the adoption of reserved-seat quotas was significantly more likely where women had served as the executive. Ireland is a great example of this. While there have been past attempts to pass national quotas in Ireland, we found that such an outcome is likely only if a significant number of parties adopt voluntary party quotas.

The Limits of Contagion

The mixed results on the influence of contagion on national quotas highlight some of the limitations of contagion's explanatory power. The adoption of a national quota is more likely in countries that are transitioning to democracy and where women have historically been underrepresented for any number of reasons. What this means is that we are trying to predict outcomes in cases that are really outliers. Countries such as Afghanistan and Iraq, which are incredibly poor countries that are moving to democracy after a major conflict, included national quotas in their constitutions. This choice was deliberate because women in these countries had historically been so disadvantaged politically, and in fact such strategies are meant to fast-track women's participation. On the other end of the spectrum, we see that countries such as France and Italy, which are highly developed socially and economically, are adopting national quotas because, despite all the advantages of development, women are still underrepresented in government. Indeed, women's lack of representation in these countries is quite surprising to scholars, who argue that there should be more women given what we know about representation.

Contagion alone cannot explain what is going on in these countries. In fact, any advances women make in political institutions in these cases may undercut the argument for a quota. As we found in the examination of compulsory party quotas, the presence of a significant number of women in the legislature or the selection of a female executive may make quota laws seem unnecessary. It is for these reasons that it is important to continue to consider other factors known to affect women's representation along with measures of contagion. Our effort here is not to supplant existing theories of women's political representation but instead to add another important factor to existing models.

Our results very clearly show the importance of these traditional influences on women's representation. We found that the level of development within a country, the existence or absence of a tradition of political participation and labor force participation by women, the type of electoral or selection system, the characteristics of the institution, and ideology all have strong and significant effects on women's representation even after the influences of contagion are controlled. The level of development in the country and women's labor force participation show the most mixed results, suggesting that, while a threshold of development or labor participation is positively associated with women's political participation, both variables can cut against women's participation when the values are extremely high or have no effect if they are extremely low.

Traditions of women's participation have more consistent effects on participation. We found that, across institutions, when the years since suffrage variable was significantly related to participation, it was positively signed. The importance of these traditions of women's political participation cannot be stressed enough. Women typically have to participate as voters if they are to develop interest and ambition to serve in office themselves or to develop the tools to understand how to participate in the political system.

Women's opportunities for participation continue to be relevant to women's participation. Where there are more seats on the bench, shared executive offices, and higher district magnitudes, we find more women participating in political office. In part, the greater number of seats provide more opportunity for smaller political actors, such as far-left parties that tend to favor women's participation more, to participate. When these left-wing parties take power, they force more conservative parties to adopt similarly favorable attitudes toward women if they are to stay politically competitive. Additionally, as small parties demonstrate the few negative consequences for allowing greater participation by women, they decrease the costs for other parties to do so, as well. The exception to this is the adoption of reserved-seats quotas in countries with high district magnitude, where men will certainly lose out to women if a quota is adopted.

Finally, despite the influences of contagion, we still found significant effects for the differences in region. Of course, the variation in region depends on the office under study. Region is unrelated to the holding of legislative office but significantly related to other avenues of participation for women. South American and African countries are quicker to elect female executives, while voluntary party quotas are adopted more quickly in Asia than elsewhere. South American countries are faster to adopt reserved-seat quotas, but Asian countries are less likely to have voluntary quotas overall.

This strong variation in region suggests that our work on understanding women's representation is not done. While region dummy variables account for any remaining differences unaccounted for by traditional influences on participation, they do not explain the variation we have uncovered. Clearly, more developed models of women's representation that reveal more of the nuances of regional differences are needed. Similarly, our data are limited to what we could find for our initial set of 159 democracies; the missing data can provide a more complete story. The same is true for extending this analysis beyond our time frame or to countries that are not democracies.

Despite the limitation of our own work, it shows strong, substantive effects for the influences of contagion on women's representation across political institutions, time, and region. We think that the impact of contagion in any given country goes beyond raising women's consciousness (though that is important) and increases women's presence in areas of government where they can fight for other women. As countries transition to democracies or consider revisions to their current political system, the adoption of quota laws, at either the party or the national level, provides new ways to increase women's participation, not only in parties and legislatures but in all political institutions. Countries cannot increase their GDP or give women the right to vote retroactively, even though these factors theoretically would increase women's participation. They do, however, have the opportunity to change public policy in clear ways that bring more women into all institutions. The question remains whether they want to really see more women participating or whether they are paying lip service to the cause. To the extent that scholars focus on the influence of contagion, along with other factors known to increase women's political participation, we can leave political elites with no way to ignore the strong, positive influence of contagion on representation.

Appendix 1

Cases in Legislative Analysis

Country	Years
Argentina	1987–2005
Australia	1966–2004
Austria	1970–2006
Bahamas	1982–2002
Bangladesh	1996–2001
Barbados	1986–2003
Belgium	1965–2003
Belize	1989–2003
Benin	1995–2003
Bolivia	1985–2005
Bosnia and Herzegovina	2002–2006
Botswana	1984–2004
Brazil	1990–2002
Bulgaria	2001–2005
Canada	1963–2006
Cape Verde	1995–2006
Chile	1993–2005
Colombia	1982–2006
Costa Rica	1982–2006
Cyprus	1991–2006
Czech Republic	1996–2006
Denmark	1971–2005
Dominican Republic	1982–2006
Ecuador	1984–2006
El Salvador	1988–2006
Estonia	1996–2003
Finland	1962–2003
France	1973–2002
Gambia	1987–1992
Germany	1976–2005
Greece	1981–2004
Guatemala	1990–2003
Guyana	1997–2006
Honduras	1989–2005
Hungary	1994–2006
Iceland	1983–2003
India	1984–2004

(continued)

Country	Years
Ireland	1965–2002
Israel	1984–2006
Italy	1963–2006
Jamaica	1983–2006
Japan	1963–2005
Korea, Republic of	1992–2004
Latvia	1998–2006
Lithuania	1996–2004
Luxembourg	1979–2004
Macedonia, the Former	1994–2002
Madagascar	1998–2002
Mali	1997–2002
Malta	1987–2003
Mauritius	1982–2005
Mexico	2000–2006
Moldova, Republic of	1998–2005
Mongolia	1996–2004
Mozambique	1999–2004
Namibia	1994–2004
Netherlands	1977–2006
New Zealand	1963–2005
Nicaragua	1996–2006
Norway	1965–2005
Pakistan	1990–1993
Panama	1999–2004
Papua New Guinea	1982–2002
Paraguay	1998–2003
Philippines	1992–2004
Poland	1997–2005
Portugal	1979–2005
Romania	2000–2004
Saint Lucia	1982–2006
Slovakia	1998–2006
Slovenia	1996–2004
Solomon Islands	1984–1997
South Africa	1999–2004
Spain	1982–2004
Suriname	1991–2005
Sweden	1968–2006
Switzerland	1975–2003
Thailand	2001–2005
Trinidad and Tobago	1986–2001
Turkey	1999–2002
Ukraine	1998–2006
United Kingdom	1964–2005
United States	1962–2006
Uruguay	1989–2004
Vanuatu	2002–2004
Venezuela	1998–2005

Appendix 2

Cases in Executive Analysis

Country	Years
Albania	2003–2006
Algeria	1989–1991
Argentina	1984–2006
Armenia	1992–2006
Australia	1964–2006
Austria	1968–2006
Bahamas	1980–2002
Bangladesh	1992–2006
Barbados	1980–2002
Belgium	1960–2006
Belize	1985–2006
Benin	1992–2006
Bolivia	1983–2006
Bosnia and Herzegovina	1997–2006
Botswana	1980–2006
Brazil	1986–2006
Bulgaria	1991–2006
Burundi	2006–2006
Canada	1960–2006
Cape Verde	1991–2006
Chile	1990–2006
Colombia	1980–2006
Comoros	2005–2006
Costa Rica	1980–2006
Croatia	2001–2006
Cyprus	1980–2006
Czech Republic	1994–2006
Denmark	1960–2006
Dominican Republic	1980–2006
Ecuador	1980–2006
El Salvador	1980–2006
Estonia	1992–2006
Fiji	1980–2005
Finland	1960–2006
France	1970–2006
Gambia	1983–1993
Georgia	2005–2006

(continued)

Country	Years
Germany	1971–2006
Ghana	1980–2006
Greece	1977–2006
Guatemala	1980–2006
Guinea-Bissau	2006–2006
Guyana	1993–2006
Honduras	1983–2006
Hungary	1991–2006
Iceland	1980–2006
India	1980–2006
Indonesia	2000–2006
Ireland	1961–2006
Israel	1980–2006
Italy	1960–2006
Jamaica	1980–2006
Japan	1960–2006
Kenya	2003–2006
Korea, Republic of	1989–2006
Latvia	1994–2006
Lebanon	1992–2006
Lesotho	1994–2006
Liberia	1998–2006
Lithuania	1992–2006
Luxembourg	1973–2006
Macedonia	1992–2006
Madagascar	1994–2006
Malawi	1995–2006
Mali	1993–2006
Malta	1980–2006
Mauritius	1980–2006
Mexico	1998–2006
Moldova, Republic of	1994–2006
Mongolia	1993–2006
Mozambique	1995–2006
Namibia	1991–2006
Nepal	2000–2001
Netherlands	1975–2006
New Zealand	1960–2006
Nicaragua	1991–2006
Niger	1994–2006
Norway	1960–2006
Pakistan	1989–1998
Panama	1991–2006
Papua New Guinea	1980–2006
Paraguay	1993–2006
Peru	1981–2006
Philippines	1988–2006
Poland	1992–2006
Portugal	1977–2006
Romania	1997–2006

Country	Years
Russian Federation	1992–2006
Saint Lucia	1980–2006
Saint Vincent and the Grenadines	1980–2005
Samoa	1990–2006
Senegal	2001–2006
Slovakia	1994–2006
Slovenia	1993–2006
Solomon Islands	1981–2006
South Africa	1994–2006
Spain	1979–2006
Sri Lanka	1980–2002
Suriname	1987–2006
Swaziland	1980–1992
Sweden	1963–2006
Switzerland	1971–2006
Thailand	1993–2005
Tonga	1981–2006
Trinidad and Tobago	1980–2006
Turkey	1984–2006
Ukraine	1992–2006
United Kingdom	1960–2006
United States	1960–2006
Uruguay	1986–2006
Vanuatu	1981–2006
Venezuela	1980–2005
Yugoslavia (1991–2002) / Serbia and Montenegro	2001–2005
Zambia	1992–1995

Appendix 3

Female Executives by Country

Country	Years	Non Interim
Austria	2004–2004	
Bangladesh	1992–2006	1
Bulgaria	1994–1995	
Canada	1993–1993	1
Chile	2006–2006	1
Ecuador	1997–1997	
Finland	2000–2006	
France	1991–1992	
Germany	2005–2006	1
Guyana	1997–1999	
Iceland	1980–1996	
India	1980–1984	1
Indonesia	2001–2004	
Ireland	1990–2006	
Jamaica	2006–2006	
Korea, Republic of	2002–2006	
Latvia	1999–2006	
Liberia	2006–2006	
Lithuania	1999–1999	
Macedonia, the Former	2004–2004	
Malta	1982–1987	
Mozambique	2004–2006	
New Zealand	1997–2006	1
Nicaragua	1991–1997	1
Norway	1981–1998	1
Pakistan	1989–1996	
Peru	2003–2003	
Philippines	1988–2006	1
Poland	1993–1993	1
Portugal	1979–1980	
Senegal	2001–2002	
South Africa	2005–2005	
Sri Lanka	1994–2002	
Switzerland	1999–1999	
Turkey	1993–1996	1
Ukraine	2005–2005	1
United Kingdom	1979–1990	
Yugoslavia (1991–2002) / Serbia and Montenegro	2002–2004	

Appendix 4

Cases in Courts Analysis

Country
Albania
Australia
Austria
Bangladesh
Belgium
Belize
Benin
Bolivia
Bosnia and Herzegovina
Canada
Chile
Costa Rica
Czech Republic
Finland
France
Germany
Honduras
Hungary
Iceland
India
Ireland
Japan
Korea, Republic of
Latvia
Luxembourg
Mexico
Morocco
Netherlands
New Zealand
Norway
Poland
Portugal
Slovakia
Slovenia
South Africa
Spain
Sweden

(continued)

Country
Switzerland
Turkey
Ukraine
United Kingdom
United States
Venezuela

Appendix 5

Parties with Quotas

Country	Party	Year Adopted
Albania	Social Democratic party	2001
Albania	Democratic Party	2003
Algeria	National Liberation Front	2002
Argentina	Justicialist Party	
Argentina	Radical Civic Union	2000
Argentina	Front for a Country in Solidarity	
Argentina	Union of the Democratic Center	
Argentina	Self-determination and Freedom	
Argentina	Democratic Party	
Argentina	Broad Front	1995
Argentina	Movement of Dignity and Independency	
Argentina	Movement of Integration and Development	2001
Argentina	Socialist Party	2002
Armenia	Union for National Self-Determination	
Australia	Australian Labor Party	1994
Austria	Austrian People's Party	1995
Austria	Social Democratic Party of Austria	1985
Austria	The Greens	1993
Belgium	Agalev	1985
Belgium	Flemish Liberals and Democrats	1985
Belgium	Socialist Party	1992
Belgium	French Christian Democrats	1986
Belgium	Left Socialist Party	1985
Belgium	French green party	2000
Bolivia	National Unity Front	2003
Bolivia	Movement with Fear	1999
Bosnia and Herzegovina	Social Democratic party	2001
Botswana	Botswana Congress Party	1999
Botswana	Botswana National Front	1994
Brazil	Brazilian Workers Party	1986
Brazil	Democratic Labour Party	1999
Brazil	Popular Socialist Party	2000
Burkina Faso	Alliance for Democracy	2002
Burkina Faso	Congress for Democracy	2002
Cameroon	Cameroon People's Movement	1996
Cameroon	Social Democratic Front	1996
Canada	New Democratic Party	1992
Cape Verde	Social Democratic	

(continued)

Country	Party	Year Adopted
Chile	Party for Democracy	1998
Chile	Socialist Party of Chile	1997
Chile	Christian Democratic Party	1996
Costa Rica	Citizen Action Party	2002
Costa Rica	National Liberation Party	1996
Costa Rica	Christian-Social Unity Party	2002
Croatia	Social Democratic party	2000
Cyprus	Movement for Social Democrats	
Czech Republic	Social Democrats	1996
Denmark	Left Socialists	1985
Denmark	Social Democratic Party	1983
Denmark	Socialist People's Party	1977
Dominican Republic	Dominican Revolutionary party	1994
Ecuador	Ecuador Rolotsista party	
Ecuador	Party of Democratic Left	
Ecuador	People's Democracy	
El Salvador	National Liberation Front Farabundo Martí	1997
Estonia	Pro Partia	
Equatorial Guinea	Social Democratic Convergence	
Ethiopia	People's Revolutionary Dem Front	
Fiji	Fiji Labour Party	
France	Socialist Party	1990
Georgia	Citizens Union	2003
Germany	The Greens	1986
Germany	Christian Democratic Union	1996
Germany	Party of Democratic Socialism	1990
Germany	Social Democratic Party	1990
Ghana	National Democratic Congress	2000
Ghana	Great Consolidated People's party	
Greece	Pan-Hellenic Socialist Movement	1974
Haiti	Socialist Party	
Hungary	Hungarian Socialist Party	1990
Hungary	Social Democratic Party	1999
Iceland	Progressive Party	1996
Iceland	United Front	2002
Iceland	Left-Green Movement	1999
India	Congress	
Ireland	Green Party	1992
Ireland	Labour	1991
Ireland	Sinn Fein Workers Party	1991
Israel	Israel Labor Party	1977
Israel	Meretz-Yachad	
Israel	Likud	
Italy	Federation of the Greens	1991
Italy	Italian Communist Party	1987
Italy	Italian Popular Party	
Italy	Italian Democratic Socialists	
Italy	Democracy is Freedom	2001
Italy	Communist Refoundation	
Ivory Coast	Ivorian Public Front	2002

Country	Party	Year Adopted
Kenya	Democratic Party	2002
Korea	Grand National party	
Korea	Democratic Party	
Lithuania	Social Democratic Party	1996
Luxembourg	Christian Socialist party	2002
Luxembourg	Green party	
Luxembourg	The Left	
Luxembourg	Labour party	1987
Macedonia	Social Democratic Union	
Malawi	Malawi Congress party	2006
Malawi	United Democratic Front	2006
Mali	Alliance for Democracy in Mali	
Malta	Labour party	
Mexico	Institutional Revolutionary Party	1996
Mexico	Party of Democratic Revolution	1993
Moldova	Christian Democratic Party of Moldova	2004
Montenegro	Social Democratic party	1999
Morocco	Socialist Union of Popular Forces	
Morocco	National Religious Party	
Mozambique	Front for the Liberation of Mozambique	1999
Namibia	Congress of Democrats	1999
Namibia	South West Africa People's Org.	1997
Netherlands	Labour Party	1987
Netherlands	Socialist Party	1975
Nicaragua	Sandinista Front for National Liberation	1996
Norway	Centre Party	1989
Norway	Christian People's Party	1993
Norway	Labour Party	1983
Norway	Liberal Party Left	1972
Norway	Socialist LeftParty /Socialist People's Party	1975
Paraguay	National Republic Association	
Paraguay	Revolutionary Fabrerista Party	
Paraguay	Dominican Revolution Party	
Philippines	Philippines Democratic Socialist Party	
Poland	Labour Union	1997
Poland	Alliance of the Democratic Left	1999
Poland	Freedom Union	1999
Poland	Green 2004	2003
Portugal	Socialist Party	1983
Portugal	Socialist Workers party	1988
Romania	Social Democratic Party	
Romania	Democratic Party	
Senegal	Senegal Socialist Party	1996
Senegal	Senegalese Liberal party	
Serbia	Social Democratic Party	2001
Slovakia	Party of the Democratic Left	1990
Slovakia	Liberal Democratic Party	1990
Slovenia	Liberal Democracy of Slovenia	1994
Slovenia	Social-Democratic Party of Slovenia	1992

(*continued*)

Country	Party	Year Adopted
South Africa	ANC	1994
Spain	Socialist Workers' Party	1988
Spain	United Left	1989
Spain	Liberal Party	1972
Spain	Socialist Party of Catalonia	1982
Spain	Initiative for Catalonia-green	1991
Spain	Republican Left of Catalonia	2004
Spain	Nationalist Galician Block	2002
Spain	Canarian Coalition	2000
Sweden	Green Party	1981
Sweden	Left Party	1987
Sweden	Swedish Dem Labor Party	1993
Sweden	Liberal Party	1972
Sweden	Christian Democrats	1987
Switzerland	Social Democratic Party of Switzerland	1988
Switzerland	Green Party	
Taiwan	Democratic Progressive Party	1996
Taiwan	Chinese Nationalist Party	2000
Tunisia	Democratic Const. Rally	2004
Thailand	Democratic Party	
UK	Labour Party	1993
Ukraine	Social Democratic Party	
Uruguay	Socialist Christian party	1984
Uruguay	Christian Democratic Party	1993
Uruguay	New Space	1998
Venezuela	Movement Towards Socialism Party	
Venezuela	Democratic Action party	
Yemen	General People's Congress	2006
Zimbabwe	Zimbabwe African National Union-Patriotic Front	

Appendix 6

Cases in Voluntary Party Quota Analysis

Country	Years
Albania	2003–2005
Argentina	1984–2005
Armenia	2000–2003
Australia	1964–2004
Austria	1968–2002
Bahamas	1988–2002
Bangladesh	1992–2001
Barbados	1980–2002
Belgium	1960–2003
Belize	1985–2003
Bolivia	1986–2005
Bosnia and Herzegovina	2001–2006
Botswana	1980–2004
Brazil	1986–2006
Bulgaria	1992–2005
Canada	1960–2004
Cape Verde	2002–2006
Chile	1990–2005
Colombia	1987–2006
Costa Rica	1980–2006
Croatia	2001–2003
Cyprus	1992–2006
Czech Republic	1994–2006
Denmark	1960–2005
Dominican Republic	1997–2006
Ecuador	1980–2006
El Salvador	1986–2003
Estonia	1993–2003
Fiji	2005–2005
Finland	1960–2003
France	1970–2002
Gambia	1983–1993
Germany	1971–2005
Ghana	2002–2004
Greece	1977–2004
Guatemala	1986–2003
Guyana	1998–2006
Honduras	1983–2001

(continued)

Country	Years
Hungary	1991–2006
Iceland	1980–2003
India	1980–2004
Indonesia	2000–2004
Ireland	1961–2002
Israel	1980–2006
Italy	1960–2006
Jamaica	1980–2002
Japan	1960–2005
Korea, Republic of	1997–2004
Latvia	1994–2006
Lesotho	1994–2002
Lithuania	1993–2004
Luxembourg	1973–2004
Macedonia, the Former	1999–2006
Malta	1980–2003
Mauritius	2001–2005
Mexico	1998–2006
Moldova, Republic of	1995–2005
Mozambique	1995–2004
Namibia	1991–2004
Netherlands	1975–2006
New Zealand	1960–2005
Nicaragua	1991–2006
Norway	1960–2005
Panama	1997–2004
Paraguay	1993–2003
Peru	2002–2006
Philippines	1988–1998
Poland	1992–2005
Portugal	1977–2005
Romania	1997–2004
Russian Federation	2001–2004
Saint Lucia	1998–2006
Senegal	2001–2001
Slovakia	1994–2006
Slovenia	1993–2004
South Africa	1995–2004
Spain	1979–2004
Sri Lanka	1990–2002
Sweden	1963–2002
Switzerland	1971–2003
Thailand	2002–2005
Trinidad and Tobago	1980–2002
Turkey	1996–2002
Ukraine	1995–2006
United Kingdom	1960–2005
United States	1960–2004
Uruguay	1986–2004
Venezuela	1993–2005
Zambia	1992–1995

Appendix 7

National Quotas

Country	Adopt Year	Type
Argentina	1991	Compulsory
Armenia	1999	Compulsory
Bangladesh	2004	Reserved
Belgium	1994	Compulsory
Bolivia	1997	Compulsory
Bosnia and Herzegovina	2001	Compulsory
Brazil	1997	Compulsory
Burundi	2005	Reserved
Colombia	1999	Reserved
Costa Rica	1996	Compulsory
Dominican Republic	1997	Compulsory
Ecuador	1997	Reserved
France	2000	Compulsory
Guyana	2006	Compulsory
Honduras	2000	Compulsory
Italy	1993	Compulsory
Kenya	2002	Reserved
Liberia	2005	Compulsory
Macedonia	2000	Compulsory
Mexico	2002	Compulsory
Niger	2003	Compulsory
Panama	1997	Compulsory
Paraguay	1996	Reserved
Peru	2001	Compulsory
Philippines	1995	Reserved
Portugal	2006	Compulsory
Serbia and Montenegro	2004	Compulsory
Slovenia	2006	Compulsory
South Korea	2004	Compulsory
Spain	2006	Compulsory
Taiwan	1997	Reserved
Venezuela	1997	Compulsory

Appendix 8

Cases in National Quota Analysis

Country	Years
Albania	2003–2006
Argentina	1984–2006
Armenia	2000–2006
Australia	1964–2006
Austria	1968–2006
Bahamas	1980–2002
Bangladesh	1992–2006
Barbados	1980–2002
Belgium	1960–2006
Belize	1985–2006
Benin	1992–2006
Bolivia	1983–2006
Bosnia and Herzegovina	1997–2006
Botswana	1980–2006
Brazil	1986–2006
Bulgaria	1992–2006
Burundi	2006–2006
Canada	1960–2006
Cape Verde	1993–2006
Chile	1990–2006
Colombia	1980–2006
Comoros	2005–2006
Costa Rica	1980–2006
Croatia	2001–2006
Cyprus	1986–2006
Czech Republic	1994–2006
Denmark	1960–2006
Dominican Republic	1980–2006
Ecuador	1980–2006
El Salvador	1984–2006
Estonia	1993–2006
Fiji	1980–2005
Finland	1960–2006
France	1970–2006
Gambia	1983–1993
Georgia	2005–2006
Germany	1971–2006
Ghana	2002–2006
Greece	1977–2006

Country	Years
Guatemala	1986–2006
Guinea-Bissau	2006–2006
Guyana	1993–2006
Honduras	1983–2006
Hungary	1991–2006
Iceland	1980–2006
India	1980–2006
Indonesia	2000–2006
Ireland	1961–2006
Israel	1980–2006
Italy	1960–2006
Jamaica	1980–2006
Japan	1960–2006
Kenya	2003–2006
Korea, Republic of	1989–2006
Latvia	1994–2006
Lebanon	1993–2006
Lesotho	1994–2006
Liberia	1998–2006
Lithuania	1993–2006
Luxembourg	1973–2006
Macedonia, the Former	1992–2006
Madagascar	1994–2006
Malawi	1995–2006
Mali	1993–2006
Malta	1980–2006
Mauritius	1980–2006
Mexico	1998–2006
Moldova, Republic of	1994–2006
Mongolia	1993–2006
Mozambique	1995–2006
Namibia	1991–2006
Nepal	2000–2001
Netherlands	1975–2006
New Zealand	1960–2006
Nicaragua	1991–2006
Niger	1994–2006
Norway	1960–2006
Pakistan	1989–1998
Panama	1997–2006
Papua New Guinea	1980–2006
Paraguay	1993–2006
Peru	2002–2006
Philippines	1988–2006
Poland	1992–2006
Portugal	1977–2006
Romania	1997–2006
Russian Federation	2001–2006

(continued)

Country	Years
Saint Lucia	1980–2006
Senegal	2001–2006
Slovakia	1994–2006
Slovenia	1993–2006
Solomon Islands	1981–2006
South Africa	1994–2005
Spain	1979–2006
Sri Lanka	1989–2002
Suriname	1987–2006
Sweden	1963–2006
Switzerland	1971–2006
Thailand	1998–2005
Trinidad and Tobago	1980–2006
Turkey	1996–2006
Ukraine	1995–2006
United Kingdom	1960–2006
United States	1960–2006
Uruguay	1986–2006
Vanuatu	1999–2006
Venezuela	1993–2005
Yugoslavia (1991–2002) / Serbia and Montenegro	2001–2005
Zambia	1992–1995

NOTES

NOTES TO CHAPTER 1

1. Zaire is included in the dataset as the Democratic Republic of Congo.

NOTES TO CHAPTER 2

1. Ironically, the first female British legislator was an American hailing from Danville, Virginia.

2. Rosenbluth, Salmond, and Thies (2006) argue that welfare-state policies disproportionately benefit women with public jobs, leading to greater political mobilization.

3. We ran the Wooldridge (2002) test for autocorrelation on all model specifications and consistently found evidence of autocorrelation.

4. Salmond (2006) argues that controlling for first-order autocorrelation potentially overcorrects for culture, biasing the effect of other variables downwards. Dropping the control for autocorrelation does increase the size of some coefficients; it also does not account for the known autocorrelation in the model. We prefer to risk overstating the effect for culture to deal with the problem of autocorrelation.

5. The pre-1974 OECD countries are primarily advanced, industrialized democracies. They include Australia, Austria, Belgium, Canada, Denmark, Finland, France, Germany, Greece, Iceland, Ireland, Italy, Japan, Luxembourg, Netherlands, New Zealand, Norway, Portugal, Spain, Sweden, Switzerland, Turkey, the United Kingdom, and the United States.

6. Slantchev (2005) created the files necessary to run Clarify using panel-corrected standard error models.

NOTES TO CHAPTER 3

1. In fact, running the models as proportional-hazards models shows that the proportional-hazards assumption is violated by a number of the independent variables. The standard correction for this violation is to interact the offending variables with the log of time (Box-Steffensmeier and Zorn 2001). The correction, however, proved ineffective, and the proportional-hazards assumption was still violated, making the choice of models without the proportionality assumption the correct model specification.

NOTES TO CHAPTER 4

1. The Austrian Administrative Court is excluded from our analysis because it is the only administrative court for which we found information.

2. While we could have included a variable for the presence of a female executive in 2010, there is so little variation on the factor that it would be unlikely to affect the results. The same is true for the number of parties with quotas. All country variables were taken from our database and represent the 2006 level for the country.

3. The three types of quotas included in our dichotomous measure are electoral quotas, constitutional quotas, and party quotas. These quotas cover legislative office or parties but not the judiciary. A country with any of these quotas is coded as having a quota for our purposes. While in other chapters we were able to disaggregate the effects of quota types, there is insufficient variation on the types here to allow for such analysis.

4. While we could have included a "mixed selection" variable instead of executive selection, collapsing all mixed systems into a single dichotomous variable was problematic. There were several different types of mixed systems, and, without a more refined measure, a single variable would have told us little about the effect of selection on women's representation.

5. Darcy and Nixon (1996) point out that the success of women in the 1946 election was due in part to the absence of incumbents.

NOTES TO CHAPTER 5

1. Here we are discussing voluntary party gender quotas that are adopted by parties themselves. These differ from compulsory quotas that are required by law. We discuss compulsory quotas along with reserved-seat quotas in the next chapter.

2. It is possible that errors in the model are correlated with individual parties. In other words, errors in terms of our predictions will be specific to particular parties. We dealt with this problem by using robust errors clustered by individual party.

3. We relied on myriad country sources to code parties.

4. We present the median and confidence intervals around the median of the simulated posterior density. We conducted 1,000 simulations to produce the posterior distribution.

5. We ran our models using a variable for vote support that coded each party with its percentage vote in the previous election minus the average vote total for all parties in the previous election. This allows us to measure the size of a party's vote relative to the average party vote in that election year. Our results were no different in terms of sign or significance for our main variables.

NOTES TO CHAPTER 6

1. In chapter 2, we showed that such quotas significantly increase the number of women in the legislature.

2. The idea of a male bias presented by Frechette, Maniquet, and Morelli (2008) contradicts much previous work that does not find such a bias (Darcy and Schramm 1977; Hunter and Denton 1986; Kelley and McAllister 1984).

3. We use data from Polity IV Project (2004) and Freedom House (2007) to determine not only democracies but also democratic transitions. Countries that move from below 6 on Polity2 or from "not free" to "partly free" or "free" on Freedom House scores between t–1 and t are coded as having undergone a transition.

4. For each model, we present the results of a likelihood ratio (L.R.) test. This test compares the results of our multilevel mixed-effects logistic regression models to a standard logistic regression model without random intercepts. A statistically significant result indicates that the inclusion of random intercepts produces different results. In both of our models, the tests are both highly statistically significant.

5. The values are the median Empirical Bayes predictions of the random effects created by our model. The values reflect the median posterior distribution of the random intercepts that include estimates from the model parameters (Rabe-Hesketh and Skrondal 2005).

6. We can also obtain statistically significant results by more than doubling the number of quota parties. For the period in our analysis here, doubling the number of quota parties increases it to six. Given that eight parties won seats in the 2002, for example, we believe that an increase to six is a significant but not completely unrealistic number.

Adams, Melinda, and John A. Scherpereel. 2010. "Variation in Women's Ministerial Representation Across Space and Time: Towards Explanations." Paper presented at the Annual Meeting of the American Political Science Association, Washington, DC, September 2010.

Alexander, Deborah, and Kristi Andersen. 1993. "Gender as a Factor in the Attribution of Leadership Traits." *Political Research Quarterly* 46: 527–545.

Allen, David W., and Diane E. Wall. 1987. "The Behavior of Women State Supreme Court Justices: Are They Tokens or Outsiders?" *Justice System Journal* 12: 232–245.

Allwood, Gill, and Khursheed Wadi. 2004. "Increasing Women's Representation in France and India." *Canadian Journal of Political Science/Revue canadienne de science* 37: 375.

Anasagasti, Miriam, and Nathalie Wuiame. 1999. *Women and Decision-Making in the Judiciary in the European Union.* Luxembourg: Office for Official Publications of the European Communities.

Andersen, Kristi, and Stuart Thorson. 1984. "Congressional Turnover and the Election of Women." *Western Political Quarterly* 37: 143–156.

Appleton, Andrew, and Amy Mazur. 1993. "Transformation or Modernization: The Rhetoric and Reality of Gender and Party Politics in France." In *Gender and Party Politics*, ed. Joni Lovenduski and Pippa Norris. London: Sage.

Arceneaux, Kevin. 2001. "The 'Gender Gap' in State Legislative Representation: New Data to Tackle an Old Question." *Political Research Quarterly* 54: 143–160.

Atkeson, Lonna Rae. 2003. "Not All Cues Are Created Equal: The Conditional Impact of Female Candidates on Political Engagement." *Journal of Politics* 65: 1040–1061.

Baldez, Lisa. 2004. "Elected Bodies: The Gender Quota Law for Legislative Candidates in Mexico." *Legislative Studies Quarterly* 29: 231–258.

Baldez, Lisa. 2006. "The Pros and Cons of Gender Quota Laws: What Happens When You Kick Men Out and Let Women In?" *Politics & Gender* 2: 102–109.

Barnello, Michelle. 1999. "Gender and Roll Call Voting in the New York State Assembly." *Journal of Women, Politics, & Policy* 20: 77–94.

Beck, Nathaniel, and Johnathan Katz. 1995. "What To Do (and Not To Do) with Time-Series Cross-Section Data." *American Political Science Review* 89: 634–648.

Beck, Thorsten, George Clarke, Alberto Groff, Philip Keefer, and Patrick Walsh. 2001. "New Tools in Comparative Political Economy: The Database of Political Institutions." *World Bank Economic Review* 15: 1–15.

Berkman, Michael, and Robert O'Connor. 1993. "Do Women Legislators Matter? Female Legislators and State Abortion Policy." *American Politics Research* 21: 102–124.

Bonomi, Genny, Giorgio Brosio, and Maria Laura Di Tommaso. 2006. "How Italian Electors React to Gender Quotas: A Random Utility Model of Voting Behavior." Technical Report 09/2006 Department of Economics. Torino: Universita di Torino.

Box-Steffensmeier, Janet M. 1996. "A Dynamic Analysis of the Role of War Chests in Campaign Strategy." *American Journal of Political Science* 40: 352–371.

Box-Steffensmeier, Janet M., and Bradford S. Jones. 1997. "Time Is of the Essence: Event History Models in Political Science." *American Journal of Political Science* 41: 1414–1461.

Box-Steffensmeier, Janet M., and Bradford Jones. 2003. "Nonproportional Hazards and Event History Analysis in International Relations." *Journal of Conflict Resolution* 47: 33–53.

Box-Steffensmeier, Janet M., and Bradford S. Jones. 2004. *Event History Modeling: A Guide for Social Scientists*. New York: Cambridge University Press.

Box-Steffensmeier, Janet M., and Christopher Zorn. 2001. "Duration Models and Proportional Hazards in Political Science." *American Journal of Political Science* 45: 972–988.

Boyd, Christina L., Lee Epstein, and Andrew D. Martin. 2007. "Untangling the Effect of Sex on Judging." *American Journal of Political Science* 54: 389–411.

Bratton, Kathleen, and Kerry Haynie. 1999. "Agenda Setting and Legislative Success in State Legislatures: The Effects of Gender and Race." *Journal of Politics* 61: 658–679.

Bruhn, Kathleen. 2003. "Whores and Lesbians: Political Activism, Party Strategies, and Gender Quotas in Mexico." *Electoral Studies* 22: 101–119.

Budge, Ian, Hans-Dieter Klingemann, Andrea Volkens, Judith Bara, and Eric Tanenbaum. 2001. *Mapping Policy Preferences: Estimates for Parties, Electors, and Governments 1945–1998*. New York: Oxford University Press.

Burrell, Barbara. 1994. *A Woman's Place Is in the House: Campaigning for Congress in the Feminist Era*. Ann Arbor: University of Michigan Press.

Burrell, Barbara. 2006. "Political Parties and Women's Organizations: Bringing Women into the Electoral Arena." In *Gender and Elections: Shaping the Future of American Politics*, ed. Susan J. Carroll and Richard L. Fox. New York: Cambridge University Press.

Bystydzienski, Jill. 1995. *Women in Electoral Politics: Lessons from Norway*. London: Praeger.

Campbell, David, and Christina Wolbrecht. 2006. "See Jane Run: Women Politicians as Role Models for Adolescents." *Journal of Politics* 68: 233–247.

Carrio, Elisa Mara. 2005. "Argentina: A New Look at the Challenges of Women's Participation in the Legislature." In *Women in Parliament: Beyond Numbers. A Revised Edition*, ed. Julie Ballington and Azza Karam. Stockholm, Sweden: International Institute for Democracy and Electoral Assistance.

Carroll, Sue. 1994. *Women as Candidates in American Politics*, 2nd ed. Bloomington: Indiana University Press.

Catalano, Ana. 2009. "Women Acting for Women? An Analysis of Gender and Debate Participation in the British House of Commons 2005–2007." *Politics & Gender* 5: 45–68.

Caul, Miki. 1999. "Women's Representation in Parliament: The Role of Political Parties." *Party Politics* 5: 79–98.

Caul, Miki. 2001. "Political Parties and the Adoption of Candidate Gender Quotas: A Cross-National Analysis." *Journal of Politics* 63: 1214–1229.

Celis, Karen. 2008. "Studying Women's Substantive Representation in Legislatures: When Representative Acts, Contexts and Women's Interests Become Important." *Representation* 44: 111–123.

Christensen, Raymond. 2008. "Societal, Electoral, and Party Explanations for the Low Representation of Women in the House of Representatives." In *Women and Legislative Representation: Electoral Systems, Political Parties, and Sex Quota*, ed. Manon Tremblay. New York: Palgrave Macmillan.

Clark, Cal, and Janet Clark. 1987. "The Gender Gap in Yugoslavia: Elite versus Mass Levels." *Political Psychology* 8: 411–426.

Clark, Janet. 1998. "Women at the National Level: An Update on Roll Call Voting Behavior." In *Women and Elective Office: Past, Present and Future*, ed. Sue Thomas and Clyde Wilcox. New York: Oxford University Press.

Clift, Eleanor, and Tom Brazaitis. 2000. *Madam President: Shattering the Last Glass Ceiling*. New York: Scribner.

Conroy, Meredith. 2007. "Political Parties: Advancing a Masculine Ideal." In *Rethinking Madam President: Are We Ready for a Woman in the White House?*, ed. Lori Cox Han and Caroline Heldman. Boulder, CO: Lynne Reinner.

Costain, Anne N. 2003. "Paving the Way: The Work of the Women's Movement." In *Anticipating Madam President*, ed. Robert P. Watson and Ann Gordon. Boulder, CO: Lynne Reinner.

Costantini, Edmond. 1990. "Women and Political Ambition: Closing the Gender Gap." *American Journal of Political Science* 34: 741–770.

Cowley, Philip, and Sarah Childs. 2003. "Too Spineless to Rebel? New Labour's Women MPs." *British Journal of Political Science* 33: 345–365.

Craske, Nikki. 1999. *Women and Politics in Latin America*. New Brunswick, NJ: Rutgers University Press.

Dahlerup, Drude. 1988. "From a Small to a Large Minority: Women in Scandinavian Politics." *Scandinavian Political Studies* 11: 275–297.

Dahlerup, Drude. 2005. "Increasing Women's Political Representation: New Trends in Gender Quotas." In *Women in Parliament: Beyond Numbers. A Revised Edition*, ed. Julie Ballington and Azza Karam. Stockholm, Sweden: International Institute for Democracy and Electoral Assistance.

Dahlerup, Drude. 2006. "Introduction." In *Women, Quotas, and Politics*, ed. Drude Dahlerup. New York: Routledge.

Darcy, Robert, and David Nixon. 1996. "Women in the 1946 and 1993 Japanese House of Representatives Elections." *Journal of Northeast Asian Studies*. 15: 3–19.

Darcy, Robert, and Sarah Schramm. 1977. "When Women Run against Men." *Public Opinion Quarterly* 41: 1–12.

Darcy, Robert, Susan Welch, and Janet Clark. 1994. *Women, Elections, and Representation*. New York: Longman.

Davidson-Schmich, Louise K. 2006. "Gender and Political Ambition Revisited: What Questions Does American Politics Research Raise for Western Europeanists?" Paper presented at the Annual Meeting of the American Political Science Association, Philadelphia, August 31–September 3.

Davidson-Schmich, Louise K. 2008. "Gender Quotas and Political Ambition: Evidence from Germany." Paper presented at the Annual Meeting of the Midwest Political Science, Chicago, April 2–6.

Davis, Rebecca Howard. 1997. *Women and Power in Parliamentary Democracies: Cabinet Appointments in Western Europe, 1968–1992*. Lincoln: University of Nebraska Press.

Davis, Sue. 1992. "Do Women Judges Speak 'in a Different Voice'? Carol Gilligan, Feminist Legal Theory, and the Ninth Circuit." *Wisconsin Women's Law Journal* 8: 143–172.

Diaz, Mercedes Mateo. 2005. Representing Women? Female Legislators in West European Parliaments. Colchester, UK: The European Consortium for Political Research Press.

Dodson, Debra. 2006. *The Impact of Women in Congress*. New York: Oxford University Press.

Dodson, Debra, and Susan Carroll. 1991. *Reshaping the Agenda: Women in State Legislatures*. New Brunswick, NJ: Center for the American Woman and Politics, Rutgers University.

Dolan, Julie. 1997. "Support for Women's Interests in the 103rd Congress: The Distinct Impact of Congressional Women." *Women & Politics* 18: 81–94.

Drewery, Gavin, and Jenny Brock. 1983. *The Impact of Women on the House of Lords*. Strathclyde, UK: Center for the Study of Public Policy, University of Strathclyde.

Duerst-Lahti, Georgia. 2007. "Masculinity on the Campaign Trail." In *Rethinking Madam President: Are We Ready for a Woman in the White House?*, ed. Lori Cox Han and Caroline Heldman. Boulder, CO: Lynne Reinner.

Duverger, Maurice. 1954. *Political Parties*. New York: Wiley.

Duverger, Maurice. 1955. *The Political Role of Women*. Paris: UNESCO.

Easton, David. 1965. *A Systems Analysis of Political Life*. New York: Wiley.

Easton, David. 1979. *A Systems Analysis of Political Life*. Chicago: University of Chicago Press.

Epstein, Lee, Jack Knight, and Olga Shvetsova. 2001. "Comparing Judicial Selection Systems." *William and Mary Bill of Rights Law Journal* 10: 7–36.

Escobar-Lemmon, Maria, and Michelle M. Taylor-Robinson. 2005. "Women Ministers in Latin American Government: When, Where, and Why?" *American Journal of Political Science* 49: 829–844.

Falk, Erika, and Kathleen Hall Jamieson. 2003. "Changing the Climate of Expectations." In *Anticipating Madam President*, ed. Robert P. Watson and Ann Gordon. Boulder, CO: Lynne Reinner.

Farrar-Myers, Victoria. 2003. "A War Chest Full of Susan B. Anthony Dollars: Fundraising Issues for Female Presidential Candidates." In *Anticipating Madam President*, ed. Robert P. Watson and Ann Gordon. Boulder, CO: Lynne Reinner.

Farrar-Myers, Victoria. 2007. "Money and the Art and Science of Candidate Viability." In *Rethinking Madam President: Are We Ready for a Woman in the White House?*, ed. Lori Cox Han and Caroline Heldman. Boulder, CO: Lynne Reinner.

Fox, Richard, Jennifer Lawless, and Courtney Feeley. 2001. "Gender and the Decision to Run for Office." *Legislative Studies Quarterly* 26: 411–435.

Fox, Richard, and Zoe Oxley. 2003. "Gender Stereotyping in State Executive Elections: Candidate Selection and Success." *Journal of Politics* 65: 833–850.

Franceschet, Susan, and Jennifer Piscopo. 2008. "Gender Quotas and Women's Substantive Representation: Lessons from Argentina." *Politics & Gender* 4: 393–425.

Frankovic, Kathleen. 1977. "Sex and Voting in the U.S. House of Representatives, 1961–1975." *American Politics Quarterly* 5: 315–331.

Frechette, Guillaume R., Francois Maniquet, and Massimo Morelli. 2008. "Incumbents' Interests and Gender Quotas." *American Journal of Political Science* 52: 891–909.

Freedom House. 2009. *Freedom in the World*. Washington, DC: Freedom House.

Freidnevall, Lenita. 2003. "Women's Political Representation and Gender Quotas—the Swedish Case." *Research Program on Gender Quotas—a Key to Equality?* Working paper, Department of Political Science, Stockholm University, Stockholm, 2: 1–32.

Freidnevall, Lenita, Drude Dahlerup, and Hege Skjeie. 2006. "The Nordic Countries: An Incremental Model." In *Women, Quotas and Politics*, ed. Drude Dahlerup. New York: Routledge.

Fulton, Sarah, Cherie Maestas, L. Sandy Maisel, and Walter Stone. 2006. "The Sense of a Woman: Gender, Ambition, and the Decision to Run for Congress." *Political Research Quarterly* 59: 235–248.

Gaidzanwa, Rudo. 2004. "Gender, Women, and Electoral Politics in Zimbabwe." *EISA Research Report*. http://www.eisa.org.za/PDF/rr8.pdf.

Galligan, Yvonne. 2005. "Ireland." In *Sharing Power: Women, Parliament, Democracy*, eds. Marion Tremblay and Yvonne Galligan. Burlington, VT: Ashgate.

Galligan, Yvonne, and Rick Wilford. 1999. "Women's Political Represenation in Ireland." In *Contesting Politics: Women in Ireland, North and South*, ed. Ellis Ward and Rick Wilford. Boulder, CO: Westview Press, 130–148.

Genovese, Michael A. 1993. "Women as National Leaders: What Do We Know?" in *Women as National Leaders*, ed. Michael Genovese. Newbury Park, CA: Sage.

Gleditsch, Henk Goemans Kristian Skrede, and Giacomo Chiozza. 2009. "Introducing Archigos: A Dataset of Political Leaders." *Journal of Peace Research* 46: 269–283.

Golder, Matt. 2005. "Democratic Electoral Systems around the World, 1946–2000." *Electoral Studies* 24: 103–121.

Gray, Tricia. 2003. "Electoral Gender Quotas: Lessons from Argentina and Chile." *Bulletin of Latin American Research* 22: 52–78.

Gruhl, John, Cassia Spohn, and Susan Welch. 1981. "Women as Policymakers: The Case of Trial Judges." *American Journal of Political Science* 25: 308–322.

Gryski, Gerald, Eleanor Main, and William Dixon. 1986. "Models of State High Court Decision Making in Sex Discrimination Cases." *Journal of Politics* 48: 143–155.

Haussman, Melissa. 2003. "Can Women Enter the 'Big Tents'? National Party Structures and Presidential Nominations." In *Anticipating Madam President*, ed. Robert P. Watson and Ann Gordon. Boulder, CO: Lynne Reinner.

Hayes, Bernadette, Ian McAllister, and Donley Studlar. 2000. "Gender, Postmaterialism, and Feminism in Comparative Perspective." *International Political Science Review/Revue internationale de science politique* 21: 425–439.

Heldeman, Caroline. 2007. "Cultural Barriers to a Female President in the United States." In *Rethinking Madam President: Are We Ready for a Woman in the White House?*, ed. Lori Cox Han and Caroline Heldman. Boulder, CO: Lynne Reinner

Herrnson, Paul, J. Celeste Lay, and Atiya Kai Stokes. 2003. "Women Running as Women: Candidate Gender, Campaign Issues, and Voter-Targeting Strategies." *Journal of Politics* 65: 244–255.

Herron, Erik, and Kirk Randazzo. 2003. "The Relationship between Independence and Judicial Review in Post-Communist Courts." *Journal of Politics* 65: 422–438.

Hettinger, Virginia A., and Christopher Zorn. 2005. "Explaining the Incidence and Timing of Congressional Responses to the U.S. Supreme Court." *Legislative Studies Quarterly* 30: 5–28.

Hirczy, Wolfgang. 1995. "STV and the Representation of Women." *PS: Political Science and Politics* 28: 711–713.

Htun, Mala N., and Mark P. Jones. 2002. "Engendering the Right to Participate in Decision-Making: Electoral Quotas and Women's Leadership in Latin America." In *Gender and the Politics of Rights and Democracy in Latin America*, ed. Nikki Craske and Maxine Molyneux. New York: Palgrave.

Htun, Mala, and Timothy Power. 2006. "Gender, Parties, and Support for Equal Rights in the Brazilian Congress." *Latin American Politics and Society* 48: 83–104.

Huddy, Leonie, and Nayda Terkildsen. 1993. "Gender Stereotypes and the Perception of Male and Female Candidates." *American Journal of Political Science* 37: 119–147.

Hughes, Melanie M., and Pamela Paxton. 2008. "Continuous Change, Episodes, and Critical Periods: A Framework for Understanding Women's Political Representation over Time." *Politics & Gender* 4: 233–264.

Hult, Karen M. 2007. "Women as Executive Branch Leaders." In *Rethinking Madam President: Are We Ready for a Woman in the White House?*, ed. Lori Cox Han and Caroline Heldman. Boulder, CO: Lynne Reinner.

Hunter, Alfred, and Margaret Denton. 1986. "Do Female Candidates Lose Votes? The Experience of Female Candidates in the 1979 and 1980 Canadian General Elections." *Canadian Review of Sociology and Anthropology* 21: 395–406.

Inglehart, Ronald, and Pippa Norris. 2000. "The Developmental Theory of the Gender

Gap: Women's and Men's Voting Behavior in Global Perspective." *International Political Science Review / Revue internationale de science politique* 21: 441–463.

Inglehart, Ronald, and Pippa Norris. 2003. *Rising Tide: Gender Equality and Cultural Change around the World.* New York: Cambridge University Press.

Inter-Parliamentary Union. 2005. *Women in Politics: 1945–2005.* Geneva, Switzerland: Inter-Parliamentary Union.

Inter-Parliamentary Union. 2006. *Women in Politics: 60 Years in Retrospect.* Geneva, Switzerland: Inter-Parliamentary Union.

Inter-Parliamentary Union. 2008a. *Women in National Parliaments Statistical Archive.* January. http://www.ipu.org.

Inter-Parliamentary Union. 2008b. *Women's Suffrage.* January. http://www.ipu.org.

Inter-Parliamentary Union. 2011. *Women in National Parliaments Statistical Archive.* February. http://www.ipu.org.

International Institute for Democracy and Electoral Assistance. 2003. "The Implementation of Quotas: Latin American Experiences." In *Workshop Report. Lima, Peru: International Institute for Democracy and Electoral Assistance.*

International Institute for Democracy and Electoral Assistance and Stockholm University. 2010. Global Database of Quotas for Women. http://www.quotaproject.org/.

Iwanaga, Kazuki. 2003. "Women's Political Representation and Electoral Systems in Japan." Paper presented at the First International Conference, "Women and Politics in Asia," Halmstad, Sweden, June 6–7.

Jalalzai, Farida. 2004. "Women Leaders: Past and Present." *Women & Politics* 26: 85–108.

Jalalzai, Farida. 2008. "Women Rule: Shattering the Executive Glass Ceiling." *Politics & Gender* 4: 205–232.

Jenson, Jane. 1982. "The Modern Women's Movement in Italy, France and Great Britain: Differences in Life Cycles." *Comparative Social Research* 5: 200–225.

Johnson, Joel, and Jessica Wallack. 2008. "Electoral Systems and the Personal Vote." http://dss.ucsd.edu/ jwjohnso/espv.htm.

Jones, Mark. 2004. "Quota Legislation and the Election of Women: Learning from the Costa Rican Experience." *Journal of Politics* 66: 1203–1223.

Jones, Mark P. 2009. "Gender Quotas, Electoral Laws, and the Election of Women." *Comparative Political Studies* 42: 56–81.

Kahn, Kim Fridkin. 1992. "Does Being Male Help? An Investigation of the Effects of Candidate Gender and Campaign Coverage on Evaluations of U.S. Senate Candidates." *Journal of Politics* 54: 497–517.

Kahn, Kim Fridkin. 1994. "Does Gender Make a Difference? An Experimental Examination of Sex Stereotypes and Press Patterns in Statewide Campaigns." *American Journal of Political Science* 38: 162–195.

Kahn, Kim Fridkin, and Edie Goldenberg. 1991. "Women Candidates in the News: An Examination of Gender Differences in U.S. Senate." *Public Opinion Quarterly* 55: 180–199.

Kaufman, Robert, and Alex Segura-Ubiergo. 2001. "Globalization, Domestic Politics, and Social Spending in Latin America: A Time-Series Cross-Section Analysis, 1973–97." *World Politics* 53: 553–587.

Kelley, Jonathan, and Ian McAllister. 1984. "Ballot Paper Cues and the Vote in Australia and Britain: Alphabetic Voting, Sex and Title." *Public Opinion Quarterly* 48: 452–466.

Kennedy, Carole. 2007. "Is the United States Ready for a Woman President? Is the Pope Protestant?" In *Anticipating Madam President*, ed. Robert P. Watson and Ann Gordon. Boulder, CO: Lynne Reinner.

Kenney, Sally. 1998/1999. "The Members of the Court of Justice of the European Communities." *Columbia Journal of European Law* 5: 101–133.

Kenny, Sally. 2002. "Breaking the Silence: Gender Mainstreaming and the Composition of the European Court of Justice." *Feminist Legal Studies* 10: 257–270.

Kenney, Sally. 2006. "Moving beyond Difference: A New Scholarly Agenda for Gender and Judging." Paper prepared for the Annual Meeting of the Law and Society Association, Baltimore, Maryland, July 6–9.

Kenworthy, Lane, and Melissa Malami. 1999. "Gender Inequality in Political Representation: A Worldwide Comparative Analysis." *Social Forces* 78: 235–268.

King, Gary, and Langche Zeng. 2001. "Logistic Regression in Rare Events Data." *Political Analysis* 9: 137–163.

Kittel, Bernhard, and Hannes Winner. 2005. "How Reliable Is Pooled Analysis in Political Economy? The Globalization-Welfare State Nexus Revisited." *European Journal of Political Research* 44: 269–293.

Kittilson, Miki Caul. 2006. *Challenging Parties, Changing Parliaments: Women and Elected Office in Contemporary Western Europe*. Columbus: Ohio State University Press.

Klingeman, Hans-Dieter, Andrea Volkens, Judith Bara, Ian Budge, and Michael McDonald. 2006. *Mapping Policy Preferences II: Estimates for Parties, Electors, and Governments in Eastern Europe, European Union and OECD 1990–2003*. New York: Oxford University Press.

Knight, Kathleen, Yvonne Galligan, and Una Nic Giolla Choille. 2004. "Equalizing Opportunities for Women in Electoral Politics in Ireland: The View of Women Members of Parliament." *Women & Politics* 26: 1–20.

Koch, Jeffrey W. 2000. "Do Citizens Apply Gender Stereotypes to Infer Candidates' Ideological Orientations?" *Journal of Politics* 62: 414–429.

Kolinsky, Eva. 1991. "Political Participation and Parliamentary Careers: Women's Quotas in Germany." *West European Politics* 14: 56–72.

Krook, Mona Lena. 2005. "Competing Claims: Quotas for Women and Minorities in India and France." Paper prepared for the General Conference of the European Consortium for Political Research Budapest, Hungary, September 8–10.

Krook, Mona Lena. 2006a. "Gender Quotas, Norms, and Politics." *Politics & Gender* 2:110–118.

Krook, Mona Lena. 2006b. "Reforming Representation: The Diffusion of Candidate Gender Quotas Worldwide." *Politics & Gender* 2: 303–327.

Krook, Mona Lena. 2007a. "Candidate Gender Quotas: A Framework for Analysis." *European Journal of Political Research* 46: 367–394.

Krook, Mona Lena. 2007b. "Quotas for Women in Elected Politics: Measures to Increase Women's Political Representation Worldwide." Paper prepared for "Towards Achieving at Least 30 Percent Participation of Women at Decision-Making Levels in Malaysia Best Practices Seminar," organized by the Ministry of Women, Family, and Community and the United Nations Development Program, Kuala Lumpur, Malaysia, December 3–7.

Krook, Mona Lena. 2009. *Quotas for Women in Politics: Gender and Candidate Selection Reform Worldwide*. New York: Oxford University Press.

Lakeman, Enid. 1976. "Electoral Systems and Women in Parliament." *Parliamentarian* 57: 159–162.

Lawless, Jennifer. 2004. "Politics of Presence? Congresswomen and Symbolic Representation." *Political Research Quarterly* 57: 81–99.

Lawless, Jennifer L., and Richard L. Fox. 2005. *It Takes a Candidate: Why Women Don't Run for Office*. New York: Cambridge University Press.

Lawless, Jennifer, and Sean Theriault. 2004. "Will She Stay or Will She Go? Career Ceilings and Women's Retirement from the U.S. Congress." *Legislative Studies Quarterly* 30: 581–596.

Leader, Shelah. 1977. "The Policy Impact of Elected Women Officials." In *The Impact of the Electoral Process*, ed. Louis Maisel and Joseph Cooper. Beverly Hills: Sage.

Lijphart, Arend. 1984. Democracies: Patterns of Majoritarian and Consensus Governments in Twenty-One Countries. New Haven: Yale University Press.

Linehan, Jan. 2001. "Women and Public International Litigation." Background paper for the Project on International Courts and Tribunals, London Meeting. http://www.pictpcti.org/publications/PICTarticles/women.pdf.

Lovenduski, Joni, and Pippa Norris. 1993. *Gender and Party Politics*. London: Sage.

Lovenduski, Jon, and Pippa Norris. 2003. "Westminster Women: The Politics of Presence." *Political Studies* 51: 84–102.

Martinez-Hernandez, Eva and Aranxta Euzondo. 1997. "Women in Politics: Are They Really Concerned about Equality? An Essay on the Basque Political System." *European Journal of Women's Studies* 4: 451–471.

Matland, Richard E. 1993. "Institutional Variables Affecting Female Representation in National Legislatures: The Case of Norway." *Journal of Politics* 55: 737–755.

Matland, Richard E. 1998. "Women's Representation in National Legislatures: Developed and Developing Countries." *Legislative Studies Quarterly* 23: 109–125.

Matland, Richard E. 2006a. "Electoral Quotas: Frequency and Effectiveness." Paper prepared for the Annual Meeting of the American Political Science Association, Philadelphia, August 31–September 3.

Matland, Richard E. 2006b. "A Generalized Theory of Quotas." Paper prepared for the Annual Meeting of the American Political Science Association, Philadelphia, August 31–September 3.

Matland, Richard E., and Deborah Dwight Brown. 1992. "District Magnitude's Effect on Female Representation in U.S. State Legislatures." *Legislative Studies Quarterly* 17: 469–492.

Matland, Richard E. and Kathleen A. Montgomery. 2003. *Women's Access to Political Power in Post-Communist Europe.* New York: Oxford University Press.

Matland, Richard E., and Donley T. Studlar. 1996. "The Contagion of Women Candidates in Single-Member District and Proportional Representation Electoral Systems: Canada and Norway." *Journal of Politics* 58: 707–733.

Matland, Richard E., and Donley T. Studlar. 1998. "Gender and the Electoral Opportunity Structure in the Canadian Provinces." *Political Research Quarterly* 51: 117–140.

Mazur, Amy G. 2001. "Drawing Lessons from the French Parity Movement." *Contemporary French Civilization* 25: 201–220.

McDonagh, Eileen. 2002. "Political Citizenship and Democratization: The Gender Paradox." *American Political Science Review* 96: 535–552.

McElroy, Gail, and Michael Marsh. 2009. "Candidate Gender and Voter Choice: Analysis from a Multimember Preferential Voting System." *Political Research Quarterly* 63: 2–13.

McElroy, Gail, and Michael Marsh. 2011. "Electing Women: Party, District, and Candidate-level Factors." Paper presented at the Annual Meeting of the Midwest Political Science Association, Chicago, March 31–April 3.

Meier, Petra. 2000. "From Theory to Practice and Back Again: Gender Quota and the Politics of Presence in Belgium." In *Democratic Innovation: Deliberation, Representation and Association*, ed. Michael Saward. London: Routledge

Meier, Petra. 2004. "The Mutual Contagion Effect of Legal and Party Quotas: A Belgian Perspective." *Party Politics* 10: 583–600.

Meinke, Scott R. 2005. "Long-Term Change and Stability in House Voting Decisions: The Case of Minimum Wage." *Legislative Studies Quarterly* 30: 103–126.

Miguel, Luis. 2008. "Political Representation and Gender in Brazil: Quotas for Women and Their Impact." *Bulletin of Latin American Research* 27: 197–214.

Murray, Rainbow. 2004. "Why Didn't Parity Work? A Closer Examination of the 2002 Election Results." *French Politics* 2: 347–362.

Myakayaka-Manzini, Mavivi. 2003. "Political Party Quotas in South Africa." Paper prepared for the International Institute for Democracy and Electoral Assistance (IDEA)/Electoral Institute of Southern Africa (EISA)/Southern African Development Community (SADC) Parliamentary Forum Conference on the Implementation of Quotas: African Experiences Pretoria, South Africa, November 11–12.

Nechemias, Carol. 1987. "Changes in the Election of Women to U.S. State Legislative Seats." *Legislative Studies Quarterly* 12: 125–142.

Newenham, Pameral. 2008. "Wallström Wants More Women Involved in Politics." *Irish Times*, November 15.

Norris, Pippa. 1985. "Women's Legislative Participation in Western Europe." *West European Politics* 8: 90–101.

Norris, Pippa. 1987. *Politics and Sexual Equality: The Comparative Position of Women in Western Democracies.* Boulder, CO: Wheatsheaf Books.

Norris, Pippa. 1993. "Comparing Legislative Recruitment." In *Gender and Party Politics*, ed. Joni Lovenduski and Pippa Norris. London: Sage.

Norris, Pippa, ed. 1997. *Passages to Power*. New York: Cambridge University Press

Norris, Pippa. 2004. *Electoral Engineering: Voting Rules and Political Behavior*. New York: Cambridge University Press.

Norris, Pippa. 2006. "Fast Track Strategies for Women's Representation in Iraq and Afghanistan.: Choices and Consequences." Paper presented at the Annual Meeting of the American Political Science Association, Philadelphia, August 31–September 3.

Norton, Noelle. 1999. "Uncovering the Dimensionality of Gender Voting in Congress." *Legislative Studies Quarterly* 24: 65–86.

O'Doherty, Caroline. 2002. "Call for Gender Quotas for Election Candidates." *The Irish Times*, March 9.

Opfell, Olga S. 1993. *Women Prime Ministers and Presidents*. Jefferson, NC: McFarland.

Organisation for Economic Cooperation and Development. 2009. Statistical database. http://stats.oecd.org/Index.aspx.

Paxton, Pamela, and Sherri Kunovich. 2003. "Women's Political Representation: The Importance of Ideology." *Social Forces* 82: 87–114.

Phillips, Anne. 1995. *The Politics of Presence*. New York: Oxford University Press.

Pitkin, Hanna Fenichel. 1972. *The Concept of Representation*. Berkeley: University of California Press.

Polity IV Project. 2004. Polity IV Dataset. Computer file; version p4v2004. College Park, MD: Center for International Development and Conflict Management, University of Maryland.

Powley, Elizabeth. 2005. "Rwanda: Women Hold Up Half the Parliament." In *Women in Parliament: Beyond Numbers. A Revised Edition*, ed. Julie Ballington and Azza Karam. Stockholm, Sweden: International Institute for Democracy and Electoral Assistance.

Rabe-Hesketh, Sophia, and Anders Skrondal. 2005. *Multilevel and Longitudinal Modeling Using Stata*. College Station, TX: Stata Press.

Randall, Vicky. 1982. *Women and Politics*. London: Macmillan.

Randall, Vicky. 2006. "Legislative Gender Quotas and Indian Exceptionalism: The Travails of the Women's Reservation Bill." *Comparative Politics* 39: 63–82.

Randall, Vicky, and Ailbhe Smyth. 1987. "Bishops and Bailiwiks: Obstacles to Women's Political Participation in Ireland." *Economic and Social Review* 18: 189–214.

Razavi, Shahra. 2001. "Women in Contemporary Democratization." *International Journal of Politics, Culture, and Society* 15: 201–224.

Reynolds, Andrew. 1999. "Women in the Legislatures and Executives in the World: Knocking at the Highest Glass Ceiling." *World Politics* 51: 547–572.

Rincker, Meg. No date. "Chapter Two: Decentralization in Context: Testing Hypotheses about Women's Representation in Poland." http://www.artsci.wustl.edu/~mrincker/Chapter%20Two.pdf.

Rosenbluth, Frances, Rob Salmond, and Michael Thies. 2006. "Welfare Works: Explaining Female Legislative Representation." *Politics & Gender* 2: 165–192.

Rule, Wilma. 1981. "Why Women Don't Run: The Critical Contextual Factors in Women's Legislative Recruitment." *Western Political Quarterly* 34: 60–67.

Rule, Wilma. 1987. "Electoral Systems, Contextual Factors, and Women's Opportunity for Election to Parliament in Twenty-Three Democracies." *Western Political Quarterly* 40: 477–498.

Rule, Wilma. 1990. "Why More Women Are State Legislators. A Research Note." *Western Political Quarterly* 43: 437–448.

Saint-German, Michelle. 1989. "Does Their Difference Make a Difference? The Impact of Women on Public Policy in the Arizona Legislature." *Social Science Quarterly* 70: 956–968.

Salmond, Rob. 2006. "Proportional Representation and Female Parliamentarians." *Legislative Studies Quarterly* 31: 175–204.

Sanbonmatsu, Kira. 2006. "The Legislative Party and Candidate Recruitment in the American States." *Party Politics* 12: 233–256.

Sauger, Nicolas. 2009. "Party Discipline and Coalition Management in the French Parliament." *West European Politics* 32: 310–326.

Sawer, Marian. 2000. "Parliamentary Representation of Women: From Discourses of Justice to Strategies of Accountability." *International Political Science Review* 21: 361–380.

Schubert, Glendon A. 1977. "Political Culture and Judicial Ideology: Some Cross-Cultural and Subcultural Comparisons." *Comparative Political Studies* 9: 363–408.

Schwartz, Herman. 1998. "Eastern Europe's Constitutional Courts." *Journal of Democracy* 9: 100–114.

Schwindt-Bayer, Leslie. 2009. "Making Quotas Work: The Effect of Gender Quota Laws on the Election of Women." *Legislative Studies Quarterly* 34: 5–28.

Schwindt-Bayer, Leslie, and Renato Corbetta. 2004. "Gender Turnover and Roll-Call Voting in the U.S. House of Representatives." *Legislative Studies Quarterly* 29: 215–229.

Schwindt-Bayer, Leslie, Michael Malecki, and Brian Crisp. 2010. "Candidate Gender and Electoral Success in Single Transferable Vote Systems." *British Journal of Political Science* 40: 693–709.

Schwindt-Bayer, Leslie A., and William Mishler. 2005. "An Integrated Model of Women's Representation." *Journal of Politics* 67: 407–428.

Segal, Jeffrey A., and Harold J. Spaeth. 2002. *The Supreme Court and the Attitudinal Model Revisited*. New York: Cambridge University Press.

Sheel, Ranjana. 2003. "Women in Politics in Japan." *Economic and Political Weekly* 38: 4097–4101.

Shevchenko, Iulia. 2002. "Who Cares about Women's Problems? Female Legislators in the 1995 and 1999 Russian State Dumas." *Europe-Asia Studies* 54: 1201–1222.

Siaroff, Alan. 2000. "Women's Representation in Legislatures and Cabinets in Industrial Democracies." *International Political Science Review* 21: 197–215.

Simon, Dennis, and Barbara Palmer. 2010. "The Roll Call Behavior of Men and Women in the U.S. House of Representatives, 1937–2008." *Politics & Gender* 6: 225–246.

Sineau, Mariette. 2008. "The Single-Member District System: The Hidden Bonus for Notables." In *Women and Legislative Representation: Electoral Systems, Political Parties, and Sex Quotas*, ed. Manon Tremblay. New York: Palgrave Macmillan.

Siregar, Wahidah Zein Br. 2006. "Women and the Failure to Achieve the 30 Per Cent Quota in the 2004–2009 Indonesian Parliaments: The Role of the Electoral System." International Political Science Association World Congress, Fukuoka, Japan. July 9–13.

Sisk, Gregory C., Michael Heise, and Andrew P. Morriss. 1998. "Charting the Influences on the Judicial Mind: An Empirical Study of Judicial Reasoning." *New York University Law Review* 73: 1377–1500.

Skjeie, Hege. 1991. "The Rhetoric of Difference: On Women's Inclusion into Political Elites." *Politics and Society* 19: 233–263.

Slantchev, Branislav. 2005. "The Political Economy of Simultaneous Transitions: An Empirical Test of Two Models." *Political Research Quarterly* 58: 279–294.

Slotnick, Elliot. 1984. "Judicial Selection Systems and Nomination Outcomes: Does the Process Make a Difference?" *American Politics Quarterly* 12: 225–240.

Smithey, Shannon Ishiyama, and John Ishiyama. 2000. "Judicious Choices: Designing Courts in Post-Communist Politics." *Communist and Post-Communist Studies* 33: 163–182.

Smithey, Shannon Ishiyama, and John Ishiyama. 2002. "Judicial Activism in Post-Communist Politics." *Law and Society Review* 36: 719–742.

Solowiej, Lisa, and Thomas L. Brunell. 2003. "The Entrance of Women to the U.S. Congress: The Widow Effect." *Political Research Quarterly* 56: 283–292.

Songer, Donald R., and Kelley A. Crews-Meyer. 2000. "Does Judge Gender Matter? Decision Making in State Supreme Courts." *Social Science Quarterly* 81: 750–762.

Songer, Donald R., Sue Davis, and Susan Haire. 1994. "A Reappraisal of Diversification in the Federal Courts: Gender Effects in the Courts of Appeals." *Journal of Politics* 56: 425–439.

StataCorp. 2009. *Stata Statistical Software: Release 11*. StataCorp LP, College Station, TX. http://www.stata.com/support/faqs/res/cite.html.

Stevenson, Linda. 2000. Gender Politics and Policy Process in Mexico, 1968–2000: Symbolic Gains for Women in an Emerging Democracy. PhD thesis, University of Pittsburgh.

Studlar, Donley, and Ian McAllister. 1991. "Political Recruitment to the Australian Legislature: Toward an Explanation of Women's Electoral Disadvantages." *Western Political Quarterly* 44: 467–485.

Studlar, Donley, and Susan Welch. 1991. "Does District Magnitude Matter? Women Candidates in London Local Elections." *Western Political Quarterly* 44: 457–466.

Swers, Michele. 1998. "Are Congresswomen More Likely to Vote for Women's Issue Bills Than Their Male Colleagues?" *Legislative Studies Quarterly* 23: 435–448.

Swers, Michele. 2002. *The Difference Women Make: The Policy Impact of Women in Congress*. Chicago: University of Chicago Press, 2002.

Tate, C. Neal. 1981. "Personal Attribute Models of the Voting Behavior of U.S. Supreme

Court Justices: Liberalism in Civil Liberties and Economics Decisions, 1946–1978." *American Political Science Review* 75: 355–67.

Tate, C. Neal, and Roger Handberg. 1991. "Time Binding and Theory Building in Personal Attribute Models of Supreme Court Voting Behavior, 1916–88." *American Journal of Political Science* 35: 460–480.

Tatolovich, Raymond, and David Schier. 1993. "The Persistence of Ideological Cleavage in Voting on Abortion Legislation in House of Representatives, 1973–1988." *American Politics Quarterly* 21: 125–139.

Tesch-Romer, Clemens, Andreas Motel-Klingebiel, and Martin Tomasik. 2008. "Gender Differences in Subjective Well-Being: Comparing Societies with Respect to Gender Equality." *Social Indicators Research* 85: 329–349.

Thames, Frank C., and Margaret S. Williams. 2010. "Incentive for Personal Votes and Women's Representation in Legislatures." *Comparative Political Studies* 43: 1575–1600.

Thiébault, Jean-Louis. 1988. "France, the Impact of Electoral System Change." In *Candidate Selection in Comparative Perspective: The Secret Garden of Politics*, ed. Michael Gallagher and Michael Marsh. London: Sage.

Thomas, Sue. 1994. *How Women Legislate*. New York: Oxford University Press.

Thomas, Sue, Rebekah Herrick, and Matthew Braunstein. 2002. "Legislative Careers: The Personal and the Political." In *Women Transforming Congress*, ed. Cindy Simon Rosenthal. Norman: University of Oklahoma Press.

Thomas, Sue, and Jean Reith Schroedel. 2007. "The Significance of Social and Institutional Expectations." In *Rethinking Madam President: Are We Ready for a Woman in the White House?*, ed. Lori Cox Han and Caroline Heldman. Boulder, CO: Lynne Reinner.

Tomz, Michael, Gary King, and Langche Zeng. 2000. ReLogit: Rare Events Logistic Regression, 2000–2002.

Tomz, Michael, Jason Wittenberg, and Gary King. 2003. "CLARIFY: Software for Interpreting and Presenting Statistical Results." Version 2.1. http://Gking.harvard.edu.

Tripp, Aili, and Alice Kang. 2008. "The Global Impact of Quotas: On the Fast Track to Increased Female Legislative Representation." *Comparative Political Studies* 41: 338–361.

Usui, Chikako, Suzanna Rose, and Reiko Kageyama. 2003. "Women, Institutions, and Leadership in Japan." *Asian Perspective* 27: 85–123.

Valdini, Melody Ellis. 2005. "Candidate Gender as an Information Shortcut: A Cross-National Analysis of the Effects of Political Environments." Paper presented at the Annual Meeting of the Midwest Political Science Association, Chicago, April 7–10.

Vega, Arturo, and Juanita Firestone. 1995. "The Effects of Gender on Congressional Behavior and the Substantive Representation of Women." *Legislative Studies Quarterly* 20: 213–222.

Vengroff, Richard, Zsolt Nyiri, and Melissa Fugerio. 2003. "Electoral System and Gender Representation in Sub-national Legislatures: Is There a National–Sub-national Gender Gap?" *Political Research Quarterly* 56: 163–173.

Verge, Tania. 2009. "Party Candidate Selection Processes and the Gender Regime in Spain." Paper presented at the European Consortium for Political Research Conference on Politics and Gender, Queen's University, Belfast, January 21–23.

Walker, Thomas G., and Deborah J. Barrow. 1985. "The Diversification of the Federal Bench: Policy and Process Ramifications." *Journal of Politics* 47: 596–617.

Wangnerud, Lena. 2000. "Testing the Politics of Presence: Women's Representation in the Swedish Riksdag." *Scandinavian Political Studies* 23: 67–91.

Wangnerud, Lena. 2005. "Sweden: A Step-wise Development." In *Women in Parliament: Beyond Numbers. A Revised Edition*, ed. Julie Ballington and Azza Karam. Stockholm, Sweden: International Institute for Democracy and Electoral Assistance.

Welch, Susan. 1985. "Are Women More Liberal Than Men in the U.S. Congress?" *Legislative Studies Quarterly* 10: 125–134.

Welch, Susan, and Donley Studlar. 1990. "Multi-Member Districts and the Representation of Women: Evidence from Britain and the United States." *Journal of Politics* 52: 391–412.

Welch, Susan, and Donley Studlar. 1996. "The Opportunity Structure for Women's Candidacies and Electability in Britain and the United States." *Political Research Quarterly* 49: 861–874.

Wenzel, James P., Shaun Bowler, and David J. Lanoue. 2000. "Citizen Opinion and Constitutional Choices: The Case of the UK." *Political Behavior* 22: 241–265.

Westergren, Sarah. 2004. "Gender Effects in the Courts of Appeals Revisited: The Data since 1994." *Georgetown Law Journal* 92: 689–708.

Williams, Margaret S. 2008. "Ambition, Gender, and the Judiciary." *Political Research Quarterly* 61: 68–78.

Williams, Margaret S. 2009. "Individual Explanations for Serving on State Courts." *Justice System Journal* 30: 37–59.

Williams, Margaret S., and Frank C. Thames. 2008. "Women's Representation on High Court in Advanced Industrialized Countries." *Politics & Gender* 4: 451–471.

Wolbrecht, Christina. 2002. "Female Legislators and the Women's Rights Agenda." In *Congressional Studies Series*, vol. 4, ed. Cindy Simon Rosenthal. Norman: University of Oklahoma Press.

Wolbrecht, Christina, and David E. Campbell. 2007. "Leading by Example: Female Members of Parliament as Political Role Models." *American Journal of Political Science* 51: 921–939.

Wooldridge, Jeffrey. 2002. *Econometric Analysis of Cross Section and Panel Data*. Cambridge, MA: MIT Press.

Wood, Rebecca. 2007. "A Framework for Comparative Judicial Selection Research." Prepared for presentation at the 2007 Annual Meeting of the Midwest Political Science Association, Chicago, April 12–15.

World Bank. 2006. *World Development Indicators*. CD-Rom. Washington, DC: World Bank.

World Bank. 2009. *World Development Indicators*. CD-Rom. Washington, DC: World Bank.

Worldwide Guide to Women in Leadership. 2009. www.guide2womenleaders.com.

Zetterberg, Par. 2009. "Do Gender Quotas Foster Women's Political Engagement?" *Political Research Quarterly* 62: 715–730.

Zimmerman, Joseph, and Wilma Rule. 1998. "A More Representative United States House of Representatives?" *PS: Political Science and Politics* 31: 5–10.

ABOUT THE AUTHORS

Frank C. Thames is Associate Professor in the Department of Political Science at Texas Tech University.

Margaret S. Williams is a Senior Research Associate at the Federal Judicial Center in Washington, DC.

The views expressed represent those of the authors and not necessarily those of the Federal Judicial Center. Author order is alphabetical. Both authors contributed equally to the manuscript.